Demystifying Diversity

Demystifying Diversity

A Handbook to navigate Equality, Diversity and Inclusion

by

Jiten Patel & Gamiel Yafai

GILGAMESH
PUBLISHING LTD

Demystifying Diversity
Published by Gilgamesh in 2016

Email: info@gilgamesh-publishing.co.uk
www.gilgamesh-publishing.co.uk

ISBN 978-1-908531-70-4
© Jiten Patel & Gamiel Yafai 2016

Images:
Images on page 4 (The Cultural Diversity Wheel) is a trade mark of
Leading Vantage Limited, and is copyright Jiten M Patel.
The Publishers and Authors confirm that every effort has been made to
source and acknowledge copyright on other images included here and
apologise for any unintended breach.

CIP Data: A catalogue for this book is available from the British Library

This book is dedicated to all those who strive for fairness and justice for all in the world

Acknowledgements

Our collective thanks and appreciation goes to everyone who made this book happen. We say, 'made it happen', because the book seemed to have written itself.

The case studies could not have come about if it had not been for the people and organisations who demonstrated their trust in us by offering case studies for inclusion. They are: Tony O'Shea-Poon (The Open University), Shorof Uddin (Microsoft), Sharon Pegg (The Co-operative), Paul Deemer and Ricky Somal (South East Healthcare NHS Trust), Kate Nash (Shell), Tina Mason (EY, previously Ernst and Young) and Claire Jamieson (E.ON).

Thank you, also, to those whose case studies we were not able to include for various reasons: Innes Wichert (IBM), Dianne Greyson (Equilibrium Mediation Consulting Ltd), and Helen Campbell (PwC), amongst others.

Our gratitude also extends to Lara Mynors, who spent her own personal time to edit the book and to Peter Horrocks CBE, for such a thoughtful foreword.

Jiten, from his side of the authorship, would particularly like to extend his personal thanks to Peter Horrocks CBE, Vice-Chancellor, The Open University, who has shown his unequivocal commitment by taking on the mantle of Sponsor of Equality, Diversity and Inclusion at the University. Being incredibly busy, he still took the time and trouble to review the book and then to produce a foreword. Erstwhile manager, on-going mentor and friend, Anne Watts CBE has been a continuous inspiration. Finally, this book would not have been possible without the support of the people who mean the world to him; Chhaya, Umesh, Payal, Nimisha, Pritesh and dear dear Saisha's indulgence and support allowed him to come so far on this most interesting, exhilarating journey.

Gamiel, for his part would like to thank particularly Mike Bickerdike who supported financially so many of his diversity initiatives; Andrew Wilson for helping write the first public speech for the Black MBA conference, Maroline Lasebikan and Neslyn Watson-Druée who truly turned on the lights. Finally, thanks are due to partner Julie, for her support and patience and son Gabe, who has taught his father so much in his short 14 years.

Any such list of thanks will overlook countless other influencers, too many to include in this brief space, but they are valued, and to them we extend our thanks and appreciation.

Jiten Patel and Gamiel Yafai, April 2016

About the Authors

Jiten Patel: An accomplished diversity and inclusion strategist, with strong experience of Public, Private, Education and Third Sectors, Jiten is Managing Director of a successful diversity consultancy, and has headed diversity and Inclusion at two international organisations. Recent awards include Diversity Champion of the Education Sector 2015, at the prestigious *Excellence in Diversity Awards*. Jiten is a skilled trainer and facilitator, often working in complex environments. Volunteer activity includes chairing and board roles of a range of charities and steering groups.

Gamiel Yafai: Having headed up the diversity practices of two of the UK's largest Recruitment Resourcing Agencies, Gamiel is now Managing Director of a highly successful diversity consultancy, supporting a broad portfolio of clients including some major UK and European organisations move from 'policy to practice', utilising a large portfolio of traditionally 'hard to reach' minority communities. He is currently Chair of a number of charities and widely promotes the benefits of volunteering as a means of developing leadership competencies.

Contents

List of Illustrations

Foreword

Diversity is a topic that affects us all, but it's also one that's complex and often misunderstood.

As a historian, I have always been interested in seeing the impact of people on the world; from the pilgrims that sailed on the Mayflower and established a whole new culture in America, to the British Empire that *ruled the seas,* leaving its mark on the world. But cultural change of such magnitude isn't consigned to the distant past; in 2008 the world was in awe at a black man being elected as President of the USA.

In over 3 decades at the BBC I saw a huge amount of change in an institution described by a one-time Director General as, "hideously white." Indeed, we have seen tremendous change through time. The pace of change, though, has perhaps never been as fast as we have witnessed in the 20th and 21st Centuries. The world has been described as a global village and we are all its citizens, despite our differences.

Demystifying Diversity broaches the subject at a very human level, providing background and theory before going on to consider what that may mean for you and me. The authors have considered the needs of everyday people, particularly those who have to manage others or run successful organisations, bringing greater understanding and increased confidence to a topic that can often confuse.

What do the terms equality, diversity and inclusion mean? Are they simply interchangeable, reflecting whatever happens to be the 'flavour of the month'? In these pages you will find examples that give greater meaning to these words, taking readers on a journey from equality to diversity and into an ideal of inclusion. If we take a football analogy, Equality is a foundation designed to create a more level playing field, where all teams and individuals have minimal disadvantage. I use the rather clunky phrase "more level" advisedly, as it reflects my belief that we cannot completely eradicate inequality, although that should always be our aim.

Diversity is about the mix of the players on that field; we wouldn't dream of making an excellent goalkeeper the striker; the goalkeeper's strength lies in protecting the goal. At the same time, would a striker be the best person to be the goalkeeper? It is likely that they could function in those roles but we would not necessarily be maximising the chances of success. Inclusion, then, is about how the diverse people on the team can work together, harmoniously, for the benefit of the team and the game. Individuals may be excellent at working alone, but can they find it in themselves to work inclusively with a range of other people who each bring a diversity of culture, strengths, skills and thinking?

Through *Demystifying Diversity* the authors bring together their wealth of experience in this field, providing practical guidance that helps to clear the fog and mysticism that often surrounds this subject. In my journey through the BBC, the BBC World Service, and more recently, through the academic corridors of The Open University, I have seen some excellent examples of good practice, but also, sadly, situations where people have not been able to achieve their full potential. Getting this right is important; not just because it's the right thing to do, but also because it makes good business sense. McKinsey, in its 2015 Diversity Report, demonstrated that organisations which have a diverse and effective leadership tend to outperform their counterparts by as much as 35%.

I very much welcome the arrival of this book. Whilst it will not guarantee that we all get it right every single time, *Demystifying Diversity* is an excellent starting point to help raise awareness amongst readers to work more effectively, both as teams and individuals, in navigating these sometimes challenging waters.

Peter Horrocks CBE
Vice-Chancellor, The Open University

Introduction

And he found himself in front of a tribunal for political correctness gone mad. "What is the world coming to, when you can't even say what you want to say, or have a joke with your colleague?" It's a dark day in the life of a workplace...

This book is about how you and others fit into this world. You may feel that there are very important people in your life, but this book is about you and your world, not just those directly involved in your life.

How do you then make sense of a multi-cultural, multi-ethnic, multi-faceted world where it appears that the rules keep changing? Survival of the fittest is a common rule in Bio-diversity. In our modern diverse world, if the same rule applies, then what does survival of the fittest look like? Have you ever struggled with getting the best out of people? Are you getting the most from your entire workforce and your customer base or service users? We may have succeeded in getting the 'best people', but does that mean we are getting the best out of them?

We therefore set ourselves the task to remove the fog (aka political correctness gone mad) around equality, diversity and inclusion. These terms are perhaps seen as being flavour of the month and many consider that this has already been achieved. Yet, even in 2011/12, we saw discrimination related tribunal pay-outs as high as £4.45m.[1] Out-of-court settlements have often been far higher and even in the millions.

Whether you are a Human Resources manager, a line manager or a customer service representative, you have to be able to interact with and get the most from your job, and as most of the working population appears to spend a large proportion of its life working or shopping, we have to interact with others all the time. How, then, do we avoid some of the pitfalls of living and working in a world that is forever changing, forever transient. We appear to have just come to an understanding about an issue concerning diversity and inclusion and, just then, it changes.... Just like the reconfiguration of the pins into another organisational face (diagram 1).

Diversity is all about difference; whether and how that difference can be harnessed effectively is a major area of debate in the workplace and in customer service.

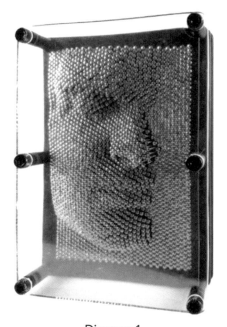

Diagram 1

Many organisations win awards for excellent diversity practice.

However, as soon as an organisation thinks, *I have cracked diversity*, there is a risk of complacency setting in. Diversity is transient and is in a constant state of flux. For example, a major facet of diversity for many in today's workforce is about the ageing population. Regardless of other facets, age and ageing affects all individuals. Currently, however, the issue is centred quite strongly on how to manage an ageing workforce where there is no mandatory retirement age. At one level, this will help as there are fewer younger people entering the workplace. At another level there are issues of ensuring that individuals are still capable. If they are not, then what will that mean in terms of the changing face of the transient nature of diversity?

Chapter 1

Identity & Culture: The Basis of Perception

You are the most important person in the world. You have dreams, aspirations, places to go and achievements to be realised. Why does the world not see this?!

To be more specific, you are the most important person in *your* world. Take a few moments to consider who you are? Did you consider yourself in terms of gender, nationality, ethnicity, social class and/or education, or were there other factors?

When you are in the majority, this question does not tend to arise so often. It becomes apparent only when seen against the light of difference. When one eight-year-old expresses no interest in football, for example, little attention is paid, but when another expresses the same opinion, eyebrows tend to be raised. The difference? The first is a girl and the second a boy.

One of the first aspects of identity that most people recognise even as early as nursery is gender. This identification with gender continues throughout schooling and into adult life. In fact, almost the first question people ask upon hearing that a friend is pregnant is, "is it a boy or a girl?" This attachment to gender is universally observed in cultures across the world. Other aspects of identity also start manifesting and being moulded as we continue to interact with family, friends and society in general.

In Diagrams 2–5, the layers that are built into an individual's identity through the cultural norms of the host community are represented in the form of *The Cultural Diversity Wheel*. In Diagram 2, the wheel shows the basic makeup of the individual. Diagram 3 illustrates the primary differentiation that, according to societal norms, is made between the individual and the 'opposite sex'. Other layers of identity then interact, along with a

The Individual – Subject to the influence of Values, Beliefs and Attitudes

Diagram 2

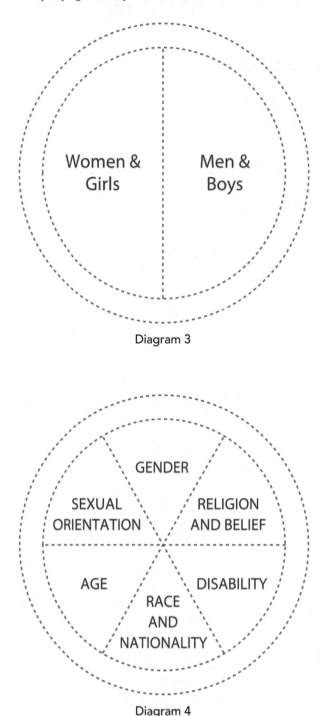

Women &
Girls

Men &
Boys

Diagram 3

GENDER

SEXUAL
ORIENTATION

RELIGION
AND BELIEF

AGE

DISABILITY

RACE
AND
NATIONALITY

Diagram 4

further layer of social conditioning (Diagram 4) and to attachments/ identities that we may not even be aware we have (diagram 5).

Beliefs, Values and Attitudes

We consider culture and cultural values to consist of a set of norms which have been accepted by a group or community. This can be seen in such popular research as Maslow's Hierarchy of Needs[2] and Morris Massey's[3, 4] research into values and socialisation, which will be explored later in this chapter. For now, we wish to consider the role of beliefs, values and attitudes in culture and identity, and in order to address this issue, it is useful to refresh our view of the meaning of these terms:

Belief: That which an individual accepts as true (such as the existence of God/a Creator). This is the individual's unique standpoint which may be shared with some people and not others.

Value: The degree of importance that someone attaches to a belief. For example, one person may value something so highly that s/he is willing to die for it. However, another may consider the same thing as far less important.

Attitude: The manifestation of a person's values and beliefs through their thoughts, words and actions. For example, a team member who appears to be obstructive and uncooperative at work may be seen as having a bad attitude.

A seemingly innocent or well-intended comment can be seen as highly offensive purely because of a mismatch of beliefs and/or values and attitudes of the people concerned. This can be seen in simple everyday communication. For example, in a department store in the West End of London, a woman asked the assistant to place her change on the counter when he offered it to her. He asked her, sarcastically, if his money was not good enough for her, not realising that her values and beliefs meant it was inappropriate to make physical contact with a male other than her husband or brothers. The same shop assistant, on seeing the disfigured hand of another customer, automatically placed the change due on the counter and was then offended when the customer asked why he had done that?

How we respond or react to situations is generally based on our beliefs, values and attitudes. This forms an integral part of our cultural and personal identity, most of which has already been constructed well before adulthood. The Jesuits even have a saying, *"give me a child until the age of seven, and I'll give you the grown man."*

Diagram 5

Levels of Prejudice

Culture and identity affect both our personal and professional lives, especially when we find ourselves in a minority within a different culture to the one in which we live and work. As discussed earlier, cultural differences can be seen even in the playground. For example, before *Harry Potter*[4a] made it *cool* to wear glasses, children who had to wear them were often ridiculed and singled out for name calling, and sometimes even suffered physical abuse. One of the authors remembers a situation in which a 40-year-old woman, when asked to recall a time at school when she had felt different, revealed that she had been dubbed "specky 4 eyes" and that even 30 years later she was still emotionally affected by the experience.

Often, in a situation where we are (or *are made to feel*) different, this causes us to question who we are, "what is our identity?" According to Gordon Allport,[5] this sense of identity creates in people a desire for acceptance and can lead them to reject others who appear to be different. Allport's research led him to recognise 5 levels of what he termed *prejudicial action*, as represented in Diagram 6 in the form of a pyramid.

1. **Antilocution:** Often as simple as name-calling, Antilocution refers to people from a majority group

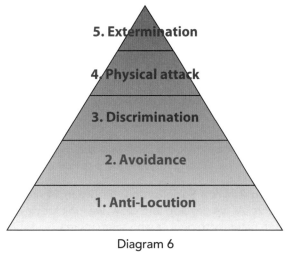

Diagram 6

freely making jokes and/or negative comments about those from a minority group. Speech is in terms of negative stereotypes and negative images. This is also called hate speech. The majority of people commonly see it as harmless. Antilocution itself may not be harmful, but it creates a foundation for more severe outlets and behaviours based on bias and prejudice.

2. **Avoidance:** Members of one group will actively avoid people in another group. No direct harm may be intended, but harm is often done through the minority being isolated.

3. **Discrimination:** Minority groups are discriminated against by denying them opportunities and services, putting prejudice into action. This is usually the level that legislation tries to address.

4. **Physical Attack:** An individual or a majority group engage in physical harm to members of the minority group.

5. **Extermination**: An individual or a majority group seeks extermination or removal of the minority group. This has often been sanitised by calling it 'ethnic cleansing.'

On a global scale, these levels were very well reported in a BBC documentary '5 Steps to Tyranny', which demonstrates how cultural identity can be a cause for people to behave in ways in which they would not ordinarily.

Conditioning brought about as a result of someone's culture and sense of identity can cause them, whether consciously or unconsciously, to establish what is important to them in their lives; in other words to establish their own value systems. Morris Massey,[6] sociologist and researcher on values and culture, conducted a whole body of research into the process of socialisation and value systems. He concluded that the core of a person's identity is often fully formed by the time they are seven years old; earlier, we alluded to the Jesuit saying 'give me a child ...." This was reinforced through research conducted by Massey, who identified the following approximate age classifications:

0 to 7 yrs – Imprinting   Up to approximately seven years old, individuals are like sponges, absorbing everything around them and accepting much of it as true (see definition of Belief, earlier in this chapter), especially when it comes from information received from their parents (whom most children of that age trust implicitly). The critical learning at this phase is the development of a sense of right and wrong, good and bad; human constructs (that are nurtured), which we, nevertheless, often assume would exist even without being nurtured. This is an indication of how deeply imprinted it has become. The core of an individual's belief and value system is considered to have been mostly formed by the end of this phase of development. Disney illustrated this point well in their depiction of Tarzan where a baby grew up with gorillas as parents. We would see real life parallels where, for example, a child (or teenager) might go into foster care and the beliefs and values of the child are a variance with those of the foster family.

7 to 14 yrs – Role Modelling   Between the ages of seven and fourteen, individuals copy other people, particularly their parents, rather than blindly accepting, they are 'trying things on', i.e. values and beliefs, to see how they feel in them. They may be greatly impressed by religion or by their teachers who seem even more knowledgeable than their parents. They may also be looking for other heroes in their lives during this phase (Nurture).

14 to 21 yrs – Socialisation   Between 14 and 21, there is a tendency to be influenced by peers. As we develop and grow, we look for ways to get away from earlier programming, and turn naturally to people who seem more like us. Other more significant influences at this stage include the media, especially when it resonates with the values of the peer group. In times

CHE GUEVARA

Diagram 7

gone by, it would not have been uncommon to see posters of Che Guevara (Diagram 7) on the walls of an aspiring university student, and in 2002, the film *Bend it like Beckham* showed an aspiring footballer surrounding herself with her hero's memorabilia (again, Nurture).

From here, people's beliefs and value systems are further realigned by their broader experiences in the workplace and by their wider social interactions, *socialisation*. Even as far back as Roman times, this process of socialisation was used/manipulated to change people's outlooks by creating what has been termed a 'Significant Emotional Event',[7] a life event that brings about a shift in awareness. For example, when one of the authors sustained a slipped disc, he suddenly had experiential evidence of what it might be like to not have mobility. Shakespeare very cleverly illustrated how this can happen, in his play, Julius Caesar; Cassius' address to the masses after Caesar's assassination ("Friends, Romans, Countrymen, I come to bury Caesar, not praise him") stirred the crowds into insurrection. This behaviour was also demonstrated in the way in which Adolf Hitler addressed the German youth of the day.

Enoch Powell's Rivers of Blood speech in Birmingham in 1968 provoked a similar reaction amongst the white majority in the UK. In terms of Allport's 5 levels, Powell's speech[8], in our opinion, can be equated to the first level of prejudicial action, *Antilocution*, described in Allport's model, which amounted to a verbal attack on immigrants in the UK in order to preserve the UK for the so called home communities. A report of his speech is given below:

"1968: Powell slates immigration policy"
Addressing a Conservative Association meeting in Birmingham, Mr Powell said Britain had to be mad to allow in 50,000 dependents of immigrants each year....
He compared it to watching a nation busily engaged in heaping up its own funeral pyre....
[He] called for an immediate reduction in immigration and the implementation of a Conservative policy of "urgent" encouragement of those already in the UK to return home....
[If not]...Like the Roman, I seem to see the river Tiber foaming with much blood."
In Context
Enoch Powell's so-called "Rivers of Blood" speech was his defining political moment.
However, thousands of workers staged strikes and marches in support of his views and he was inundated with letters from well-wishers.
In 1968 he predicted that by the year 2000, up to seven million people living in Britain would be of [minority] ethnic descent.
The Census in 2001 showed 4.6 million people living in the UK were from an ethnic minority, or 7.9% of the population."
It is a relatively small step for a significant minority to move from a level two position, (distancing yourself from those who are less desirable, to level 3, *Discrimination* (e.g. to remove those who are perceived to be a problem). *Discrimination* is the level that is addressed by equality legislation.

Prejudice Played Out

Here, we want to discuss the reality of perception. Consider, for example, someone who has anorexia; despite others telling them they are too thin, their personal reality is that they are not thin enough. There is relatively little research available about men who are anorexic[9], and commonly the condition is associated with 'young' women. As a result women are more likely to be seen in a negative light because they are deemed to be susceptible to the condition. A person's repeated thoughts and beliefs start to be established and ultimately ingrained into their own experience and perception of themselves and others.

Driven by unfounded fears (such as those expressed, for example, in Enoch Powell's speech), within the workplace there is often a perception that equality, diversity and inclusion are only about creating disadvantage for your average white male in favour of individuals from minority/disadvantaged groups. This is portrayed in the mass media as being all about *giving them something for nothing.* If we take the example of *Springboard*[10] (a women's development programme designed originally for the BBC, and which has now been used successfully by over 180,000 women world-wide), a common complaint raised in organisations where it was introduced was *"why is there not a similar programme in place for men."* This issue has been addressed in Chapter 6, *Educate or Legislate*, under *Positive Action*.

There is also another very common perception that equality, diversity and inclusion can work only in certain environments. An often-quoted classic example here is a construction site where there is a predominance of white working class men. Often, those involved consider that women cannot manage such a construction site workforce effectively. It is likely that the only reason this perception took on the face of reality was because, historically, it was alien for women to be in the workplace at all, let alone one such as a construction site. As late as the 1970s, female students were often advised to take administrative/secretarial jobs by their careers advisors. Women were still not considered as the mainstay of a successful business economy. Such stereotypes were often reinforced through soap operas and comedy shows such as *Love thy Neighbour* or *On the Buses,* where *Olive* was seen to be stupid by her brother and husband, and needed to be supported by them. In modern day Britain, women are still seen largely as primary carers of children and home-makers. Maybe this is why there is still a dearth of top women Board Directors, perhaps owing to unconscious bias and socialisation about the role of women in the workplace.

When faced with situations that appear to threaten an existing status quo, it is often felt to be easier to stick to *the devil you know rather than the devil you don't.* How easy would it be for a blind person to describe what a rose looked like? Similarly, it is not easy for someone who takes a commonly held stereotypical stance and has never experienced discrimination to understand its impact on those who have. Equally, those against whom discrimination is perpetrated sometimes fail to recognise it as such, because it has become an accepted part of the norm. Often the experience of blatant discrimination is easily identified. However, the more subtle forms, conveyed through a look, feeling or careless expression, can go easily undetected. Then, a significant emotional experience can trigger a reaction, e.g. the effect of *Stop and Search* on young black people, or, historically, Emily Pankhurst fighting for the Suffragette Movement, challenging the accepted situation that only men had a right to choose the Government.

History of Migration to the UK[11]

Let's just take a look at why ethnic diversity, due to inward migration, in the UK is not a recent phenomenon...

40,000-30,000 BC ~	The first Europeans may have been hunter-gatherers who followed a route from North Africa. However, genetic data has recently shown that the DNA of Western Europeans resembles that of the people of India, suggesting that an inland migration from Asia seeded Europe.
6,500 BC ~	The English Channel was formed. The British Isles were colonised by Celt and Pict tribes.
43 AD ~	The Romans invaded Britain, bringing with them four legions and about 20,000 auxiliary troops, predominantly from France, Germany and Eastern Europe.
410 AD ~	Having penetrated as far as Cornwall, Wales and the Humber, Roman troops finally left Britain after 400 years of occupation.
5th Century AD ~	Romans were replaced by settlers from the German regions of Angel and Saxony, the Anglo-Saxons. They brought their own language, which gave rise to the English spoken today. Jutes and Frisians from Denmark were also settling in the British Isles.
11th Century AD ~	The Anglo-Saxon period lasted for approximately 600 years, coming to an end in 1066 with the Norman Conquest. In common with previous settlers, the Normans brought with them their early French language and culture, which fundamentally changed the direction of the English language, government and law. During the Medieval period the first Jewish people were invited to settle in England to develop commerce, finance and medicine.
13th Century AD ~	The Jews were expelled and were followed by new waves of migrants, including German merchants and Italian bankers.
16th Century AD ~	1560, Dutch Protestants fleeing religious persecution made their way to Britain.
17th Century AD ~	1685, religious persecution forced 100,000 Huguenots to flee France to the British Isles, bringing with them skills such as silk weaving, clock-making and gun making. Black slaves, many from the Caribbean, began appearing in households in the UK as a result of the slave trade.
19th Century AD ~	Merchants expanded the slave trade and increased the number of Africans living in the UK. After the 1798 Rebellion, many Irish people fled to Manchester. Irish men were frequently employed in the construction of new canals. Irish women worked as domestics and street vendors. Further Irish migrants fled to the UK in the 1840s due to the Great Famine. Many Irish women worked in the mills while the men worked on the canals and railways.

Late 1800s and early 1900s ~	Following the abolition of the African slave trade, some wealthy families brought Indian servants to Britain. Small numbers of professionals from India, mainly doctors, businessmen or lawyers, also started to establish themselves in Britain. Black and Chinese seafarers started settling around some British ports. In 1892, Britain's first non-white MP, Indian Dadabhi Naoroji, was elected. South Shields became home to Yemenis since the 1890s. Many arrived, working on board British merchant vessels. Similar communities were established in Hull, Liverpool and Cardiff. 1909 saw the first Yemeni Boarding House in the Holborn riverside district of South Shields.
1930s, 1940s and 50s –	Following the Second World War, there were significant labour shortages. 157,000 Polish people were among the first groups to be encouraged to settle in the UK (the Eastern European phenomenon is not just a latter-day occurrence); they were followed by other displaced persons from Italy, Ukraine and Germany. Many Eastern Europeans sought refuge in the UK following the establishment of Communism. The partition of India in 1947 was the starting point for greater migration and settlement of people from South Asia (due to the demise of the British Empire and to the right of British subjects to settle in the Britain).
The Windrush ~	On 22 June 1948, the Empire Windrush docked at Tilbury in London, delivering hundreds of men from the Caribbean. Mass migration to the UK continued over the following years; the National Health Service and organisations like London Transport recruited many men and women from the Caribbean. This period also witnessed a migration from the Indian sub-continent, where many Indian soldiers had fought for Britain and the Alliance in the Second World War. The invitation to migrate to the UK came from Britain in order to help address acute labour shortages and assist with rebuilding the country in the wake of two world wars.
1960s ~	Kenya attained independence from British rule and this affected countless British subjects of Indian origin. Faced with the prospect of political instability and the risk of losing jobs and businesses, such British subjects were then faced with the daunting choice of remaining in Kenya, returning to India, although they no longer held Indian citizenship or coming *home* to the UK.
1970s ~	80,000 Asian Africans were expelled from Uganda in 1972, many of whom held British passports. Of these, 28,000 were admitted to the UK.
1980s ~	Large numbers of Australians, New Zealanders and South Africans moved to the UK. This was the time when apartheid was being seriously challenged with many individuals and businesses boycotting certain British banks that continued to operate in South Africa
1990s ~	Ethnic conflict in the Balkans forced thousands to seek asylum in the UK.
2000s ~	EU member states have access to work opportunities throughout the EU. This enabled skilled and talented individuals from Eastern Europe to make themselves available on a competitive basis to the demands of UK consumers.

Blue & White Collar

Traditionally, blue collar and white collar workers are thought of as describing factory workers and office workers, respectively. For our purposes and in recognition of the diversity of business and industry sectors, let us consider white collar as describing those roles that involve all tiers of management, and blue collar as describing all other more junior roles. Regardless of role and perhaps much more based on upbringing and the influence of the media, it's easy to see how people can very quickly develop stereotypical views about different individuals and communities. Please consider the words in Diagram 8 and make a mental note of the terms people might most commonly associate with them.

Asylum seeker	**Barbie doll**	**Blackboard**
Coloured	**Dumb**	**Gay**
Gypsy	**Immigrant**	**Jew**
Terrorist	**Wheelchair bound**	**White**

Diagram 8

In Diagram 9, we provide a list of terms we have come across during our experience of this arena, that are commonly used to describe those words. You may wish to consider them against your own mental list. It can be seen that the majority of the terms are emotive and negative. These, very often unconscious perspectives can then influence people's behaviour towards others even where they would not consciously intend to discriminate or offend. A court case, *Moore vs. Transport For London and others (29 Sep 2004; ET/2302017/2003)* recognised the principle of unconscious discrimination and bias. Of course, it needs to be borne in mind that bias can be both positive and negative. For example, one candidate may be selected over another because the recruiter feels more comfortable with them in a given role. But that may be the result of unconscious bias in favour of the less suitable candidate.

Asylum seeker	Barbie doll	Blackboard
Immigrant	Blonde bimbo	Why can't I say this anymore?
Illegal	Stupid	PC gone mad
Sponger	Good looking & Brainless	
Free-loader		
Coloured	**Dumb**	**Gay**
Mugger	Stupid	Queer
Back of the lorry	Downs Syndrome	Not normal
Paki	Slow	Well groomed
Fresh off the boat	Incapable	Camp
		Dyke
Gypsy	**Immigrant**	**Jewish**
Trouble maker	Taking our jobs	Yid
Unclean	Jumping the queue for	Tight Fisted
Litterbugs	council houses	Skull Caps
Thieves	Social security frauds	Successful
	Loads of children	
Terrorist	**Wheelchair bound**	**White**
Islam	Restricted	Normal?
9/11	Poor them	Privileged?
Al Qaeda	Incapable	?
Fundamentalist	Dependant	?

Our experience in using this exercise with many groups has shown that when 'white' people are asked to find stereotypes to describe themselves they found it quite difficult to fill in the gaps.

Diagram 9

Blue collar/white collar becomes very relevant when thinking about whether your organisation is representative of the population. For example, there have been situations where an organisation has demonstrated that it employs a diverse workforce, but the diversity is most predominant amongst its blue collar population. Commonly related experiences tell us that those aspiring to management may well hale from a variety of backgrounds, but those achieving promotion are still more likely to be white, male and middle class. Sometimes, this is a function of the nature of the industry or sector, where, for example, there may be relatively little staff turnover and so opportunities are not so readily available, e.g. the British Armed Forces.

In such situations, as has been observed, for example, with the British Army, it takes a concerted effort on the part of the organisation to consciously *and persistently* work towards creating a diverse and effective workforce throughout its hierarchy.

In the next chapter, we continue to explore the more practical implications of culture and identity and how they play out in terms of first impressions and stereotyping.

Chapter 2

Perception is Reality

*I reach conclusions by reviewing facts, weighing evidence and analysing arguments.
I only wish others did the same! I mean, let's face it, we are being overrun by migrants
and they're taking all our jobs. I read it in the paper; they are spongers and just taking
advantage of our social security system!!*

This concept that a person's perception is their reality has been verified many times over and is often seen as the basis of both positive (e.g. *all Asians are family-orientated and look after their elders*) and negative (e.g. *all black people are muggers; all disabled people can't work*) stereotyping. In the extreme, this has led to the idea of 'political correctness gone mad' and feeds unconscious bias, a topic we will discuss further in Chapter 10.

In our opinion, sensationalism of a few instances (often extensively publicised in the media under highly emotive headlines) can then discourage noble and well intended actions. Sometimes, in an effort to appear inoffensive, good intentions can lead to actions that provoke extreme reactivity and bad press. This can give rise to accusations of political correctness gone mad, owing to misunderstandings due to oversimplification of issues. For example, it was reported that a UK school had asked parents to encourage the multi-cultural ethos of the school by supporting the sending of greeting cards for different festivals (i.e. Eid and Diwali) but then wrote to parents asking them not to send Christmas Cards in the December of the same year in case it was offensive to Muslim and Hindu families. We wonder which of these actions was political correctness gone mad.

Even as far back as 2003, the BBC reported that The Red Cross had banned Christmas nativity decorations from its UK charity shops in case they offend customers of other Faiths. One volunteer, Christine Banks, was dismayed to be told to remove a nativity scene from the window of the Kent shop in which she worked.

She said it was political correctness gone mad and leading British Muslim Labour peer Lord Ahmed said it was "stupid" to think other Faiths would be offended by Christian symbols.

The Red Cross reported that it believed an alignment with a particular religion could "compromise our ability to work in conflict situations around the world," and yet there is an equivalent relief agency called the Red Crescent. It is interesting to observe that the Red Cross and the Red Crescent have been affiliated since 1919.[13] Whilst there have been international debates about the appropriateness of each of their logos (a cross symbolising Christian and crescent symbolising Islamic backgrounds) for international relief efforts, ultimately they stand side by side today. In its efforts to collect charitable donations, The Red Crescent does not, to our knowledge, discourage the celebration of Eid or the use of Muslim symbols.

Language, tradition and culture are organic and move with time. If we consider this, in the light of the diagram 10, perhaps it will help to make sense of how terminology also moves with the passage of time, perception and experience.

A history of Politically Correct language

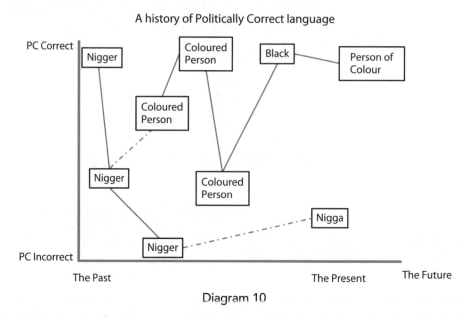

Diagram 10

Depending on who you are and your perspective, different terms will invariably be at different points on the continuum; this is often a function of the impact that identity and culture has on us. Some words or actions deemed offensive by certain groups or individuals are viewed by others as political correctness gone mad. The difference in perspective often lies in misunderstanding context. You would only have to do a Google search on the term Baa Baa Black Sheep to see the confusion surrounding this one term.

> *This is not the first time, however, that the nursery rhyme — written in 1744 satirising the taxes imposed on wool exports — has fallen foul of political correctness. In 2000, Birmingham City Council tried to ban the rhyme after claiming that it was racist and portrayed negative stereotypes. The council rescinded the ban after black parents said it was ludicrous.*

The Times, March 6th, 2006

In the same way, because language moves with time, it can be difficult to keep up with the refinements, which on the one hand can lead to a fear of offending others (do I say Black/Coloured/Person of Colour?…*Help!*), and on the other hand can create a culture where there is a need to *fit in* with the majority, or so-called *'in' group*. In Allport's model (the 5 levels of prejudicial action), he contends that the first level of prejudice is *Anti-locution* (See Chapter 1, Diagram 6); perhaps better known to us as name calling and often initiated as early as nursery or kindergarten. Anti-locution often is used as part of initiation 'rites' when a person joins a new team or new organisation and gets ascribed a nick-name which can be done as a joke or to ridicule the new member of staff. Whilst there may be no malicious intent, the name chosen for the person can leave him or her feeling vulnerable and/or singled out for inappropriate attention. For example, a worker in a public service organisation was dubbed 'Mick' by his colleagues, a reference to his Irish origin (in this case it was *thick Mick*). When he complained about this, his manager told him that "the lads don't mean anything by this; it's just a bit of harmless fun and you really need to grow a thicker skin if you want to work here."

Here, maybe the colleagues concerned intended no offence and had ascribed nicknames to each of their team members, but to our minds they had failed to take into account the cultural context surrounding the name given to this individual. This was further compounded by the person in a position of power (white collar) dismissing the issue as superficial by dismissing the complaint when it was raised; somehow (and perhaps unconsciously) the complaint was dismissed as political correctness gone mad.

Often in the workplace, people are faced with situations that end up being classified as political correctness gone mad. *Political correctness gone mad* as an absolute term, we feel, is meaningless and only acquires meaning when seen against different contexts. Often, accusations of political correctness are an extreme reaction to a situation where someone has found themselves in front of overzealous Diversity & Equality police. For example, it is reputed that as a response to criticisms of institutional racism, the Metropolitan Police issued booklets consisting of words and terms that officers could and could not use. Often, when something does not fit neatly with a person's personal world view, as determined by their traditions, religion, attitudes and culture, they may seek to view it as alien and/or as political correctness gone mad.

TRACC®14

TRACC represents Tradition, Religion, Attitude, Culture and Community, all of which impact on you and your response to life and work. If we were to take this a step further, culture is often used as an all-encompassing word for all of TRACC. We decided to break down culture and arrived at the following equations:

- Culture = Beliefs x Values x Experiences x Expectations
- Community (and even Corporate) Identity = Culture x Socialisation x Institutionalisation

TRACC can be seen as an extension to Allport's model in that it sits below the Pyramid we presented in Chapter 1, Culture and Identity – The Basis of Perception. It is often positioned as the virtual 90% of the iceberg that sits below the surface level and feeds the conditioning that each of us undergoes from, if not before, birth. The analogy of a tree comes to mind; big oak trees come from small acorns. The acorn germinates and the tree grows. The roots often go far deeper and wider than the part of the tree we see above ground level. The effects of TRACC may be thought of as the trunk, branches, leaves, flowers and fruits of the tree. However a larger part of the nutrients required for growth come from under the ground. Our contention is that, similarly, in society and workplace culture, what we see is words and actions or behaviours that are apparent to all. What feeds those behaviours is often rooted deep in the unconscious mind and consists, in part, of the labels you see under the ground level in Diagram 11. Clearly these labels are not exhaustive. If the tree does not receive the appropriate nutrients, it will produce poor quality, bad, or no fruit. If the unconscious is feeding the behaviour through inappropriate beliefs and values, the resulting actions (fruits) may well lead to discrimination.

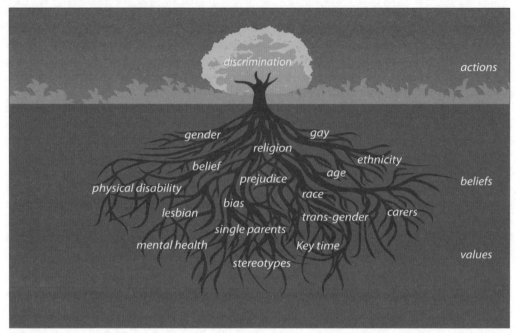

Diagram 11

Discrimination, in Law, is an action based on inappropriate behaviour which, itself, is predicated by our beliefs and values and cannot necessarily be seen as they are below the surface level and often deeply embedded.

Diagram 12

Many times, there is no desire on the part of the individual to deliberately discriminate; it results from bias that is lodged in our subconscious (unconscious) beliefs and value systems.

When in Rome...

How often have you heard the phrase 'When in Rome, do as the Romans do'?

To what extent should you be expected to conform to things which are alien to you and which may be totally contrary to your whole belief system? For example, in the UK it is a given that Christmas is a national holiday to celebrate the birth of Jesus Christ. Even academic calendars work around the festival of Christmas. Nobody is expected to sit an exam on Christmas day. The one day of the year in the UK that newspapers don't get printed is Christmas day. Should only those that practice various forms of Christianity be given the day off? Taking this a step further, why should people from other faiths have to sit important exams during important festivals in their respective calendars; is it simply because when in Rome...?

When we think about *when in Rome*, it is useful to think, too, what this phrase meant originally. The phrase originated in Rome, and Rome was wherever the Romans were, i.e. the Roman Empire. We could also, on this basis, consider that, at the time when she ruled the seas, Britannia expected everybody in the British Empire to do as the Britons did. However, in the time of Queen Victoria, whilst Black and Asian people were a part of UK life perhaps mingling and inter-marrying were still, nevertheless, unthinkable at that time; (i.e. to marry someone who was from a minority community, a white Briton would need to think of someone from the incoming community as equal in status)

Given these norms, it has often been expected that new communities simply *do as the Romans* (assimilate). It does also beg the question of who could not *do as the Romans did*? The slaves and the Christians; they were not expected to mingle with the Romans and inter-marrying was unthinkable. We wonder who the slaves and Christians of the 20th and 21st Century are in the UK and around the world?

Integration versus Assimilation

This brings us on to the issue of degrees of inclusion in UK life and work. In our view, assimilation can be seen as expecting the arriving culture to be subsumed by the host culture almost immediately. Integration, on the other hand, can be seen as the two cultures peacefully coexisting and interchanging. Over a period of time, such integration can lead to so many similarities that they could almost be deemed as mutual assimilation

It is this intervening period that can be a cause of contention and can build up a resistance which translates into an unconscious bias and institutionalised discrimination. This will be covered in more detail in the chapter 10 which will cover unconscious bias.

Since the late 1970's, (following the arrival of Indians post 1973, after their expulsion from Uganda by Idi Amin), much political focus has gone in to trying to reduce the number of inward migrants. Membership to the EU of newer European States, and access to UK Public services by members of those States has also been seen as unjust by the host communities. Often, relatively small scale incidents of 'abuse' of the UK's social security and health services has caused people to brand whole communities as undesirable residents. There is also a commonly held view that, "if you come here you should be like us" – Assimilation.

As seen earlier in this chapter inward migration has long been a part of UK culture. Often, when incoming communities found jobs in the UK, it tended to be work that was undesirable to the host communities, e.g. in the cotton mills in the North, the steel industry in Sheffield, the coalmines and foundries of the *Black Country* (is the term "Black Country" politically incorrect?), in auxiliary work in hospitals and such like. Additionally, such people were mocked as being uncivilised because *they lived 10 to a room*. Again, there were reasons - a family would have made a great sacrifice to send its son to a foreign country and the son would have felt the cultural responsibility to support his family – and to do that he was willing to sacrifice the luxury of a three-bedroomed semi in favour of sharing one room with several others so that he could then support his family back home; a sheer contrast to more traditional perspectives in outlook in the western world. Here we can see how TRACC comes into play.

If we look at TRACC in terms of the UK workplace today, where workforces may appear to be representative, proportionality[15] still does *not* exist; a significant proportion of working people from minority communities are often to be found in manual, semi-skilled, auxiliary positions but not in management or executive roles. To a large extent, this also applies to women. The Chartered Management Institute in the UK reported that, "Analysis of the 2015 National Management Salary Survey of 72,000 UK managers reveals that women working in equivalent full-time roles earn 22% less than men, meaning that they're unpaid for 1h 40m a day – a total of 57 working days every year." Disabled people are perhaps not even on the radar.

Whilst this is changing, progress is slow. Most of the FTSE 250 companies and all of the Public Sector bodies in the UK now have some form of Equality, Diversity and/or Inclusion statement incorporated into policy. Many have taken *Initiatives*, under *Positive Action* permissions given by UK and European equality legislation, to develop individuals from disadvantaged groups in order to create better representation in their respective workplaces.

Inclusion is very much centred on the principal of integration, and while there is still a need for *Initiatives*, in the workplace, to re-adjust proportionality in the light of historical disadvantage, we can assume safely that integration has not yet been achieved. Change is uncomfortable. Nonetheless, there is still a fear that persists amongst people about their own sense of security, which feeds certain media appetites to add fuel to the fire. This sense of fear is not just limited to indigenous communities, but even extends to newer communities in the UK who feel threatened by subsequent new communities arriving. We have seen much in the press about Polish people and Eastern European communities. One of the authors has been privy to conversations amongst Indian communities about *all these Somalis taking over!* However, this does not stop "Britons" employing the services of people who are offering more value for their money at the cost of jobs for UK citizens.

Integration also needs to be differentiated from insulation and assimilation, all of which are affected by TRACC and can be considered in terms of diagram 13. In order to better understand this diagram, we could use the example of a meal:

Insulation: When all the ingredients for our recipe are separately distinguishable and identifiable and do not mix with each other, often stored separately.

Integration: If those ingredients were turned into a three-course meal, the ingredients are working together to create a set of tasty complementary dishes.

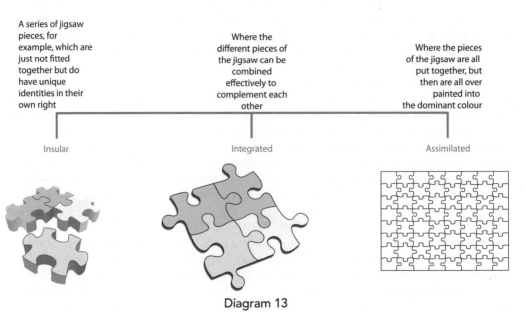

Tradition, Religion, Attitude, Culture, Community
A Question of Degrees

A series of jigsaw pieces, for example, which are just not fitted together but do have unique identities in their own right

Where the different pieces of the jigsaw can be combined effectively to complement each other

Where the pieces of the jigsaw are all put together, but then are all over painted into the dominant colour

Insular

Integrated

Assimilated

Diagram 13

Assimilation: However, if the ingredients were just added in to the same pot indiscriminately and blended together, the final result may very well be uninteresting at least and perhaps toxic at worst.

Or, to simplify this further, imagine bowls, each containing different fruits (*insulation*), compared to a fruit salad (*integration*). If the fruit salad was 90% apples and 10% other fruits and you blended it all, the bulk of the flavour and texture would be apples (*assimilation*). We will talk more about workplace integration in the chapter 3, *You and the People you work with*.

Nature versus Nurture

There are many different definitions of nature and nurture and ideas about their impact on issues of equality, diversity and inclusion.

For our purposes, the physicality of gender and certain disabilities, as well as where a person is born, can be assigned to nature. However, *how* these facets are then understood and applied could be assigned to nurture. In the world of biodiversity, the principal of survival of the fittest predominates; if you are not fit enough in any sense of the word, then the likelihood is that you will perish. By way of example, in the jungle a mother with a wounded cub would likely abandon the cub to its fate. A human mother would be very unlikely to do this, and that has allowed the world to witness such phenomena as Steven Hawking, Robert Oppenheimer and Marie Curie. In biodiversity, Hawking would have been left to be eaten by predators, Oppenheimer would have had no regrets about creating the Atom Bomb, and Marie Curie would not have been concerned about saving victims of war

It is widely accepted that the human condition goes beyond biodiversity to a state that we have termed *Socio-diversity*.[16] Socio-diversity accredits humanity, amongst others, with the principals of compassion, integrity, dignity, respect and sustainability; all of which appear in one guise or another in workplace policy commitments. In the world of work, we have often heard the phrase 'dog eat dog', and yet that appears to be contrary to the way in which communities and cultures have developed internally. It could be argued, therefore, that the natural human condition is one of mutual support and common progress, but only when you look like me, talk like me and behave like me. This was seen in Gordon Allport's principal of 'in' groups (See Chapter 1). One of the authors recollects a conversation where a person was discounted for a senior post because that person did not pick up cutlery *in the right order* during a banquet.

Such common purpose alters more towards biodiversity when different societies are vying for supremacy over others, as seen in the Roman conquests, Alexander the Great's empire building, both world wars and regional/territorial situations such as the Settlers against the Native Americans, the Australians against the Aborigines, the Arabs against the Israelis, the English against the Irish, and so on. In more recent times in the UK, the debate has revolved around participation in the European Union and the so-called *flood of Eastern Europeans threatening local jobs and local businesses*.

These debates, however, often centre on the fringes of inclusion, where individual and very often negative situations tend to be unconsciously branded as the norm relating to a particular group of people, usually via media sensationalism from which political advantage can then be extrapolated. Such perspectives are then carried into the world of work, manifesting in ill-informed attitudes.

In an ideal world scenario, no intervention of any sort would be required, as there would be no imbalances if the principles of Socio-Diversity were at the heart of Strategy, Policy-making and Operations in every workplace and in every community and in every family. Sadly, we do not live in an ideal world.

Corporate cultures, it can be seen, tend to be fashioned on TRACC and influenced by political structures. Corporate leaders, who may have spent years, even decades, building up their business may well feel much more comfortable with people who look like them, talk like them and behave like them, as perhaps do we all. This will be covered in more depth in Chapter 3, *You and the people you work with*. However, what is often missed is the contribution made by newer and minority communities to the fabric of the host communities. For example, HSBC started a South Asian Banking Unit in about 1998 in the UK with one office, and this was expanded to somewhere approaching 10 units within 5 years. Not only was this profitable to HSBC because they were able to utilise a broader range of cultural expertise, it also then contributed to the UK tax coffers.

Diagram 14

Chapter 3

Employment – *You and the People You Work With*

Once upon a time, two people were looking for a job. Charley and Manjit both had qualified with a 2.1 honours degree from the same university. They both applied for very similar jobs and Charley found a role that was well suited and offered great career prospects. Six months later, when Charley and Manjit met, Charley was surprised to hear that Manjit had still not found work.

Most organisations may be unaware of how many customers/potential employees may be deterred from applying because they feel they will not be accepted without having to change a part of who they are. By way of example, there was a very bright graduate trainee recruited by a company in the FMCG (Fast-Moving Consumer Goods) sector who, as part of his graduate development, was posted to a store in a somewhat remote rural area. Shortly after this placement, the individual resigned from this major high street name. Upon further enquiry, it was found that the individual in question did not feel a sense of belonging. The company in question then needed to hire a new recruit which entailed more management time and cost. We will come back this employee later in this chapter.

In recruitment circles, professional recruiters are often cautioned to be aware of the 'horns and halo' effect. This is where we have the potential to unconsciously evangelise those similar to us and demonise those who appear to be different from us. Many of us will have heard the phrase, 'better the devil you know...'. In business and in public service we all wish to minimise our risks and maximise potential; we want the best people. This does not mean that the best people are clones of ourselves; very often, having a range of skills and talents in a team adds value to our businesses and in service provision. If, for example, a football team only bought strikers how well would the team defend against the opposition's strike force.

In order to employ the right people it is essential to set objective criteria against which to assess applicants. The authors have often come across situations where 'objective criteria' has not been written to reflect the requirements of the role but to the specification of the desired individual.

The Employment Cycle

Most employees spend between 3 and 12 hours per day, doing waged or salaried work. In fact, next to sleep, it is accepted that most of us spend more time at work than doing anything else. For many of us, this routine starts when we are as young as 13 (delivering newspapers, for example) and will continue until we retire. This state of affairs is often referred to as the Employment Life Cycle or the Employment Cycle.

Whilst the terminology varies, most professionals would tend to consider the employment cycle in terms of the following key areas;

Attraction	Selection	Recruitment
Retention	Promotion	Termination

In addition, effective working and customer service requires that our working demographic be effective in achieving the aims and objectives of the organisation. This requires an ability to draw from the widest pool of available talent that reflects the diversity present in the marketplace.

Our intention here is to demystify the way in which equality, diversity and inclusion affect the above key areas of the employment cycle. It is useful to consider whether a recruiter appoints the right person to the right post at the right time; also, whether someone, as an employee, feels they are the right person in the right post at the right time. Furthermore, someone's status as the 'right person' may well be affected by their age, disability, race, religion, sex, sexual orientation or other facets and individual circumstances.

Here below we consider the components of the employment cycle and the dynamics of the people you need to work with and provide a service to.

This diagram should not be considered in isolation, but read in conjunction with subsequent paragraphs of this chapter.

Most organisations claim to be meritocracies,[17] in which all individuals are allowed to achieve their full potential, and yet we have come across innumerable situations in which individuals have felt that they were overlooked (perhaps deliberately) and equally large numbers of managers who felt helpless when trying to manage their underperforming staff effectively, for fear of being branded as an 'ist'[18] (sex-ist, Rac-ist, etc).

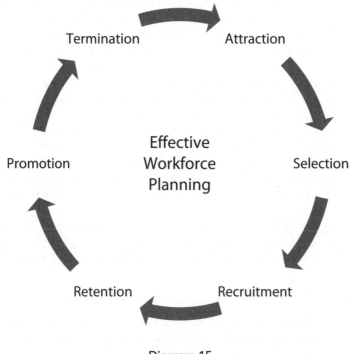

Diagram 15

Historically we have seen a situation where, in like-for-like work, women have been paid an average of 11–22%[19] less than their male counterparts. Often, this was justified simply by changing the job title, and was reinforced through a typically very British convention of deeming it inappropriate and positively uncivilised to discuss pay and salary levels/awards with colleagues, or anybody, for that matter. Let's go back to the stages we identified in the employment cycle.

Attraction

Attraction is the process of identifying and encouraging applications from the broadest pool of talent available and potentially willing to join the recruiting organisation. It is in an Organisation's interest to be able to select from the most appropriate/best qualified individuals to undertake the role/function for which a vacancy exists.

History shows us that attraction has often been restricted to a few select outlets. For example, it is an established fact that many of the FTSE 100 companies have an 'A' list and a 'B' list of universities from which they prefer to draw their candidates. This status quo itself presents a challenge, as it tends to perpetuate the recruitment of 'clones', i.e. individuals whose outlook and behaviour emulates that of the recruiting organisation. Whilst there is an argument to say this is not a bad thing, it can also lead to an elitist positioning whereby creativity and innovation can be stifled. The justification used for such positioning is often based around the need to maximise restricted budgets. However, research done by the University of Coventry showed that students who were accepted having achieved low grades at 'A' level often outperformed students who had achieved higher grades. Furthermore, it is to be noted that universities in the so-called 'B list' often have a far more diverse population than the more traditional, or Russell Group universities. It is this level of recruit that will often end up in the senior ranks of an organisation.

When we start looking at broader areas of employment, a number of factors come into play in terms of how individuals are attracted to certain jobs and/or industries. For example, it is well known that the Fire and Rescue services have, in the past, employed three generations of *men* from the same family. The same can be said of the Print, Rail, Steel and Mining industries. Although the situation is changing, when we consider nursing and nursery teaching, for example, it is still the case that these industries are attracting significantly more women than men. In retail, it can be seen that the pool of recruits tends to be very wide ranging, but then again, this diversity tends not to be reflected higher up in those organisations. The same can be said for UK-based call centres.

A question that comes to mind when considering the subject of attraction is how people may be attracted to different types of job. Often, when considering a job, the underlying factors prevailing in most peoples' minds are their need for financial self-sufficiency, the proximity of the job to home and their personal/family circumstances. It would be common, therefore, to find students and/or mothers of young children working an evening or night shift at a call centre. Often such jobs tend to be sourced from places such as employment agencies or via word of mouth where the job seeker has a friend or family member working in the given organisation. In the case of people searching for careers, their search for work may well start with looking at vacancies advertised in the so-called quality newspapers and related websites.

By its very nature, attraction needs to be targeted for reasons of both finance and access to appropriate talent. However, there is an inherent danger here of lapsing into a state of complacency that fails to take account of the changing demographics in this (now) global marketplace. It becomes necessary to ensure that procedures and practices are reviewed regularly to allow the workforce to represent the customer/stakeholder base. In the past, it was common practice to simply place an advertisement in the minority publications and assume that that was sufficient to attract people from diverse backgrounds. Our experience has shown that this approach is a good way to raise awareness of the employer brand, although, in our experience, yields relatively little in terms of conversion to new recruits. We have found that, for the more professional roles, individuals not traditionally associated with that role are just as likely as someone from the majority community to research it through traditional recruitment routes. The differentiator will often prove to be the content and tone of the advert itself. In a range of cultures, there is a traditional pecking order of preference for different types of role which can look similar to the following (this is not an exhaustive list):

- Doctor
- Lawyer
- IT Professional
- Engineer
- Accountant
- Banker

When individuals from minority communities who are suitably qualified in one or other of the above areas find little employment opportunity available, they will often turn to some form of self-employment. This is often driven by a need and a desire to be self-sufficient and not dependent on the State. According to Multi-Cultural Communications (MCC), Weber Shadwick's in 2010 "...specialists net disposable income generated by BME communities in the UK is estimated at around £70bn."[20]

> Key message: Effective targeting creates an inclusive and effective workforce

Selection

Selection is the process whereby those expressing interest in a job following their attraction to it are then 'tested' for their suitability to effectively carry out the work required for the role. This leads to a job offer.

The most commonly known selection tool is the interview. Interviews can be both formal and informal; sometimes even just a formality. History shows us that it is common for recruiters to be more comfortable with individuals who look like them and behave like them than with those who do not. This approach, as has been proven many times, can often lead to a whole organisation becoming almost clone-like. This viewpoint is exemplified very beautifully by Perry the Peacock,[21] and goes a long way towards explaining the lack of diversity, particularly at Board-level within an organisation. In the book, the peacock is not able to be itself amongst everyone else in the office who are penguins.

In order to make selection effective for both the prospective appointee and the organisation, it needs to be objective and to take into account both the actual and potential competency of an individual to undertake the role to be filled. This can be accomplished in a number of ways; the prerequisite would be to ensure the role is clearly defined and then to identify appropriate skills needed to be able to fulfil the clearly-defined role. The role requirements should be reviewed regularly, especially in such a rapidly changing environment as has been seen in the workplace since the 1980's and the IT revolution.

The role of the assessor becomes crucial to fair and objective selection. Often, assessors are individuals who may eventually be line managing the successful candidate(s) and, in the absence of appropriate recruiter training, the result could well be *recruitment in my own image*,[22] which would not necessarily see the right person being placed into the right post at the right time. Many large organisations have in-house recruiter training programmes, but it is surprising that, whilst they think they *have* done so, diversity and inclusion has often not been addressed effectively enough as an *integral* part of such training.

> Key message: Recruiting 'in my own image' only creates clones. Objective selection improves productivity and creativity to our changing marketplace.

Recruitment

Often, recruitment is thought of as the whole process of finding people to work for a company or become a new member of an organisation.[23] More accurately, this is the whole *recruitment process* and if we consider the term *Recruitment* on its own, strictly speaking, it occurs at the point where a job offer is made and accepted. This entails the process of contractually or informally engaging a person to become an employee or member of the organisation. It is often witnessed by an employment contract signed by both the new appointee and the organisation.

When recruitment is informal or by inference/implication (for example, when a person assumes or claims they are working for, or on behalf of, an organisation and the organisation, knowing this, takes no corrective action), it can lead to a number of misunderstandings and disparity between individuals within the organisation. It may also be a precursor to some form of unlawful discrimination. A principal reason behind this is that the informal recruit is very likely to have been selected on the basis of an affinity with the recruiter rather than through fair and objective selection. For example, a person may have had a 'pub chat' with their friend and invited the friend to become a trustee on the board of a local charity.

> Key message: Be wary of 'a friendly chat', because you may be held to account in a tribunal because of it. Document your selection and recruitment procedures and ensure assessors are familiar with them.

Retention

This is the process whereby the individual becomes integral to the organisation through induction, leadership, team building, training and development, motivation and, of course, remuneration.

There was once an idea of a job for life, where a person started in one organisation and stayed there until they retired. In the more recent employment environment, it is recognised that an individual will typically work for 3 or 4 organisations or even more during their working lifetime. It has been shown that it can cost up to 18 months' worth of a person's remuneration package just to recruit them. As a result, it becomes important for an organisation to be able to maximise its investment in the recruitment process by recruiting the right individuals and retaining them for as long as possible. This can be achieved in a number of ways. Money is not always a primary reason for retention. Retention relies on an individual feeling *valued* by their employer, and often it has been shown that staff will accept lesser remuneration/perks when they are happy in their work and their workplace.

Retention issues can arise when managers do not have the appropriate skills to manage all employees on a fair and objective basis. Often line managers have been unable to draw a distinction between a person's performance and issues arising from their perception of the person's status as belonging to one or more of the 9 protected characteristics (Age, Disability, Gender reassignment, Marriage and Civil Partnership, Pregnancy and Maternity, Race and ethnicity, Religion and Belief, Sex (gender) and Sexual Orientation) as defined by the Equality Act 2010. By way of example, in a recent investigation it became apparent that the line manager had gone straight to formal proceedings with a person who was from a minority ethnic background (around an issue of lateness) rather than having an informal conversation with the person first. In a similar situation involving a white employee the manager simply spoke to the person concerned and resolve the matter. As a result, the Black employee resigned and raised a claim for discrimination. It transpired that the only reason the manager went to formal procedure was to avoid appearing to be racist in addressing the lateness issue.

Our experience tells us that, in the absence of effective Equality and Diversity training, managers are fearful of accusations of racism or discrimination. Such fear then paralyses the manager from taking action to address performance issues affecting staff from minority groups until such point as they can no longer be ignored and become subject to formal procedures. By this time it is almost too late to manage issues more pragmatically and may result in losing the employee.

> Key message: In the new world order there is no such thing as a job for life. If you want to keep the best people, make your organisation inclusive and provide adequate diversity awareness training to ensure that managers develop both technical and cultural competence to manage their staff.

Promotion

This is the process of providing recognition and additional responsibility/power to individuals identified as suitable for 'upward' progression in the company/organisation. Promotion is often accompanied by increments in remuneration and other perks.

Many people have a desire to move upwards in their organisation and often this is facilitated by recognition of a person's technical skills when advancing them through an organisation. Often, this causes issues in the organisation because it is recognised generally that as an individual moves higher and higher in an organisation, the balance of the required skills shifts away from technical and more to people related skills. This is represented visually in Diagram 16.

In an ideal world, organisations would be meritocracies where, everybody has the same opportunity for career development as long as they have the skills and competence to undertake the role. However, it is interesting to note that even after centuries of migration to the UK, the majority of Senior and Executive Management teams are still largely 'White' and largely male, even though the workforce of 'UK plc' is approximately 50% female. This is often where the organisational culture and invisible rules come into play. For example, in a recent piece of research, which involved one of the authors, management was categoric that all vacancies were open to all suitably qualified staff. The detailed research showed that whilst all vacancies were advertised on the company's job circular on its intranet, it was often the case that certain individuals tended to receive a lot more positive encouragement to apply than others (often in the form of informal 'chats' at the

Diagram 16

coffee machine, etc). We noted that the individuals who progressed were not always the 'best' or 'brightest', but the ones who had better interpersonal relationships with their line managers and other senior figures in the organisation. These sort of situations can be seen as relating to the invisible rules of playing the organisation game that may not always be familiar to 'outsiders'.

When considering your employee profile, it will be useful to take note of whether you might be accused of having installed a glass ceiling; i.e. something that allows you to see through to the top but prevents you from reaching it. Glass ceilings, in our opinion, can be attributed to the influence of unconscious bias which then manifests in attitudes amongst the organisations' leadership. Such bias tends towards promoting certain groups of individuals whom they deem as suitable to get into the lift which takes you through the glass ceiling. Some such suggestions are that:

- you are a woman with children, and so unable to give the required commitment and dedication to a top level position
- You will not be able to "fit in" as a leader of said organisation. In our circuits with organisations we often hear potential recruits must be able to 'fit into the team'. We would refer you to our earlier discussions about creating clone-like cultures; they can often stifle creativity and business innovation.
- If you are a graduate from an Ivy League or Russell Group University, you must be good and hence leadership material compared to if you went to a newer ("B list") University.
- If you have not hit senior management by the age of 35, then you must be 'over the hill'.

The UK Coalition Government, elected in 2010, stated that it wished fairness rather than bureaucracy to be the premise for all equality legislation. Such an aim is laudable, although local custom and practice suggest that we are far away from this ideal when looking at the state of the UK workplace today. It is only when organisations become accountable that they tend to take action appropriate to the challenge of becoming inclusive. This, of necessity, requires a certain amount of bureaucracy until such time as it is 'business as usual' and integral to working practice and customer service.

> Key message: The only acceptable form of discrimination is on the basis of ability to do the job. It is wrong (and we use the word 'wrong' deliberately) to promote someone simply to reflect a different organisational demographic if the person promoted does not have the skills to do the job. It is great to have aspirational targets about workforce diversity, but these are often seen as quotas to be filled and are then detrimental to business success.

Termination

This is where an individual leaves their job/organisation. This could be instigated either by resignation, promotion, retirement, summary dismissal or, sadly, death, etc.

Termination is always ideal when it is by mutual agreement of both employer and employee. In the past, this often occurred at retirement. This, of course, is likely to be a big challenge with the removal of a mandatory retirement age and in the absence of objective justification (ie, where unlawful discrimination is deemed to be a proportionate response by an employer/ service provider to a legitimate business reason – cost cannot be a sole consideration under objective justification). It is acknowledged that there is a shrinking 'working age' population (commonly recognised as those aged between 18 and 65 years), which means that termination may be more likely to occur (initiated by an employee) as employers compete for the most coveted talent.

Often, termination occurs in less than ideal circumstances. People have said that they would resign from a job rather than raise a grievance about issues they have experienced. Whilst HR contends that a part of its function is to support the workforce, invariably it appears that in the case of performance and/or grievance issues, a common perception persists that HR support tends to favour the establishment above the individual. For example, a simple search on the internet will reveal a plethora of examples of how individuals feel they have been treated less favourably than the management/establishment. Of course, it is also fair to say that people often will go to HR only as a last resort, and, the role of HR is to be impartial and to provide appropriate advice and guidance to all parties. Clearly, HR professionals can handle situations in a much better way if they had been made aware of potential issues at the earliest opportunity. Most HR published employee handbooks will have a section about dignity and respect. It is unfortunate that individuals would often rather leave than raise a complaint.

This area is covered extensively by the Employment Tribunal Service, which is in place to adjudicate on issues where no employer/employee conflict resolution can be reached. Many cases going to tribunal concern harassment, bullying and victimisation, all of which are accepted as forms of discrimination at law. Whilst this is covered in more depth in chapter 6 (Educate or Legislate), it is worthwhile noting that there is no upper limit to damages awards that can be decided by tribunals.

However, there is still today a common perception that people in their 40's are often unemployable and have far more difficulty finding work if they have been made redundant, especially if they are not in senior management by this age. It makes us wonder at the perhaps outdated adage 'life begins at 40'! This perspective is now being challenged as organisations are employing staff beyond the traditional retirement age of 60–65.

> Key message: We are in an increasingly competitive marketplace where there is no job for life, and 'last in, first out' is not a viable option. Neither is losing all of your corporate history through voluntary early retirements. It is as important to terminate objectively as it is to attract, select, recruit, retain and promote.

You may be wondering about our graduate trainee and why he resigned from a potentially very promising career.....

Where he was posted, there were no other people from his own cultural or religious background. He often felt that he was being stared at by customers and colleagues alike. He was given a hard time by his parents for not visiting home frequently enough (travel costs were prohibitive). He felt alone, alienated and unsupported by his employer.

Whilst the employer may well have got attraction, selection and recruitment right, this example highlights how retention failed and became a cause for termination.

Often employers wish to be exemplary and to be seen as role models of good practice. In the case above, consideration was given only to the technical development of the trainee. It is not easy for a person to bring only a part of himself or herself to the workplace. Where a person is conflicted in this manner then it is common to see performance eroded. It is necessary therefore to ensure that workforce planning and strategy take account of the individual as well as the role/skills needs of the organisation. This makes it essential to undertake regular monitoring, evaluation and support activities.

Monitoring

There is a common phrase in management circles, 'if you cannot monitor it, you cannot manage it'. Monitoring for diversity and inclusion is not, as is commonly believed, about filling quotas. It has been proven on many occasions that the most successful organisations tend to employ workforces and develop products/services that are reflective of their stakeholders (e.g. customers, shareholders, investors, service users). This was done most successfully in the late 90's and early 2000's by B&Q who pioneered reasonable adjustments such as portable hearing induction loops, and demonstrated the benefits of employing a more mature workforce profile.

Needless to say, if such organisations had not been aware of how their workforce and customer base was comprised they would not have been in a position to undertake effective target marketing or to fill roles through the appropriate application of diversity and inclusion.

Evaluation

Whilst monitoring is a prerequisite for any organisation wanting to be inclusive, such monitoring will only prove useful if there is effective evaluation of any data that has been collected. We are aware of many organisations that have reams of information that simply sit on someone's top shelf or in their bottom drawer. Monitoring allows us to design and implement strategies to assist with our business aims and objectives. Once such strategies are in place, it becomes crucial to assess their effectiveness regularly and to take corrective action as required. People may be thought of as the liquid assets of the business; too much cash in a non-interest-bearing account yields no return. Not enough cash in a working account may incur a financial cost. Similarly, if the right people are not employed in the right parts of the business, that business is not performing at its optimum and potentially not maximising on the business advantages this would bring.

Support

People are very often confused about how to make diversity and inclusion an integral part of work and customer service. This is where it becomes important to put appropriate levels of support in place to maintain the workforce at all levels of the employment cycle. For example, when considering retention and promotion, line management would need practical training to ensure objective selection takes place that meets both the needs of the organisation and takes account of appropriate talent/competency; length of service is no longer a guarantee of promotion.

Effective support is also crucial where issues of bullying, harassment and victimisation may be experienced by employees. Often, those in a position of power may confuse bullying, harassment and victimisation with strong management. Clearly, in these circumstances there would have been a failing on the part of the organisation to ensure that staff had been trained appropriately.

Chapter 4

Creating Common Understanding

Seeing the headline in the newspaper, Bob's mother was incensed that her son was being accused of involvement in seedy gang culture when all he was doing was claiming his right to his own rich heritage…

How often do you consider whether your style of communication is effective and, more importantly, *appropriate* to a given context or situation? Communication is something we all seem to do most of the time without necessarily giving it much thought; rather like breathing, it is something we don't pay much attention to until we have a problem with it. What are the implications for this in your work and/or for your business?

A little exercise for you to do: Take a look at the following brand names. What do they communicate to you?

- MacDonalds
- Boots
- Tesco
- Starbucks
- Next
- Dominos
- Thorntons
- Mothercare
- Marks and Spencer

How many of them, would you say, champion equality diversity and inclusion? Extracts from their respective websites about their statements on Equality, Diversity and Inclusion are given below:

MacDonalds

"Our culture: a job with us offers a culture of flexibility, opportunity, equality and development. Our employees come from all walks of life, but share a common approach: positivity."[24]

Boots

"Within the United Kingdom… our culture, working patterns and buying habits continue to change rapidly alongside our changing demographics. Our family and societal norms are also changing dramatically and probably more rapidly than many anticipated.

We fully understand that it's essential for us to attract and retain diverse employees and customers from all sectors of the community if we're going to remain competitive.

We serve the whole community, and our ability to respond to the needs of all our customers is clearly enhanced if our own community within Boots UK is equally diverse. Recruiting, retaining and promoting diverse employees is critical to our success in this rapidly changing marketplace.

Of the people we employ, over 12% come from ethnic minority backgrounds. However this is not reflected at all levels in Boots UK and work continues to address this. We have diversity policies relating to gender, race, religion, belief, age, disability and sexual orientation. These policies are constantly reviewed in light of changes in legislation and best practice, as well as the changing demographics and make-up of our society."[25]

Tesco

"Everyone is welcome.

Our success depends on people and we're all different and diverse.

We believe we can't afford to be complacent around diversity issues and are continually working on initiatives to attract people from all backgrounds.

We aim to employ people who reflect the diverse nature of society and we value people and their contribution, irrespective of age, sex, disability, sexual orientation, race, colour, religion or ethnic origin.

We also try and make sure everyone can work in a way that suits their circumstances - we support flexible working, offering part-time roles and encouraging job-sharing opportunities and shift swapping where possible."[26]

Starbucks

"Aside from extraordinary coffee, Starbucks has made a business out of human connections, community involvement and the celebration of cultures. We're committed to upholding a culture where diversity is valued and respected. So it's only natural that as a guiding principle, diversity is integral to everything we do.

At Starbucks we define Diversity in the form of an equation – Diversity = Inclusion + Equity + Accessibility

Inclusion: human connection & engagement

Equity: fairness & justice

Accessibility: ease of use & barrier free

Our company-wide diversity strategy focuses on four areas: partners, customers, suppliers and communities.

Partners (our employees) - We seek out and engage partners who are as diverse as the communities we serve. Focusing on partner development by educating and engaging our partners."[27]

Next

"To encourage a successful business it is important we are able to create an environment that enables us to attract and retain the right people to work at every level throughout Next who are committed to working together, and who support our business approach of honesty, respect and encouragement.

Our people are a valuable asset to Next, and we are committed to providing a working environment in which our employees can develop to achieve their full potential and have opportunities for both professional and personal development."[28]

Dominos

"Domino's Pizza is an equal opportunity employer committed to the development of positive policies to promote equality of opportunity in employment. Our aim is to ensure that no job applicant or employee receives less favourable treatment on the grounds of sex, marital status, race, colour, creed, ethnic origin, sexual orientation, religious beliefs, age or disability."[29]

Thorntons

"Thorntons PLC is intent on ensuring equality and diversity as key features within all its activities. Equality and diversity are essential factors that contribute to a professional organisation.

Thorntons PLC believes that excellence will be achieved through recognising the value of every individual. We aim to create an environment that respects the diversity of staff, and enables them to achieve their full potential, to contribute fully, and to derive maximum benefit and enjoyment from their involvement. Thorntons acknowledges the following basic rights for all:

- to be treated with respect and dignity
- to be treated fairly with regard to all procedures and assessments
- to receive encouragement to reach their full potential
- to be provided with a safe, supportive and welcoming environment

No individual will be discriminated against. This includes, but not exclusively, on the basis of gender, race, nationality, ethnic or national origin, religious or political beliefs, disability, marital status, social background, family circumstance, sexual orientation, gender reassignment, spent criminal convictions, age, or for any other reason. We aspire to recruit, motivate, develop and retain outstanding people who work together harmoniously toward common business objectives."[30]

Mothercare

"We believe that our people make our business what it is today. We are committed to equal opportunities and to being a parent-friendly company. It's hard work at Mothercare but we try to make it fun and demonstrate our commitment to our people."[31]

Marks and Spencer

"Here at Marks & Spencer we have a diverse range of employees and are committed to an active Equal Opportunities Policy. This doesn't just cover our recruitment and selection procedures, but runs right through training and development, appraisal, promotion opportunities and eventually to retirement."[32]

How well do you think your own company or organisation is communicating its commitment and dedication to equality, diversity and inclusion? When we did our random research on the brand names above, it took two hours just to uncover the statements we have cited from their respective websites, and we knew what we were looking for! Clearly, these organisations have made a commitment. Our question would be, *how easy is it for the everyday person (whether a customer or an employee) to recognise this commitment?* The National Literacy Trust research report of December 2008 shows that 1 in 6 adults in the UK population has the literacy level of an 11-year-old. Keeping this in mind it becomes increasingly important to ensure that all our communication is effective, and in order to be effective it needs to be inclusive, possibly meaning that every 11-year-old should be able to comprehend it.[33] Easier to say than to do!

Equality or Equity?

Let's consider the word *equality*. It seems to mean different things to different people. How often have you heard someone say, "I treat everybody the same," or, "When I look at you I don't see the colour of your skin"? Treating everybody the same is not the same as treating everybody equitably. It can lead to some, perhaps many, having an unfair advantage. For example, if an employer expects all employees to use the same toilet facilities, it might be preventing a whole group of disabled but otherwise very competent employees from working for that employer because they need to be treated differently in order to be afforded the same opportunity as their non-disabled counterparts. The argument raised, often by small and medium sized businesses is that legal impositions, such as having an accessible toilet, are crippling to their business. What is perhaps often forgotten, or not communicated, is that employers were given at least 10 years to make such reasonable adjustments; such adjustments are a benefit, not only to employees, but customers, too. There is nothing in UK legislation that says a person without a disability cannot use an accessible toilet. So, in actuality, a small business need only provide a toilet which is accessible by everybody.

How often has the way someone dressed, or the way they looked, communicated something to you? Why?... When someone says hello to you, what does it communicate to you? Perhaps the answer to that question is that *it depends*. Whilst communication is not an exact science, we all do it, perhaps ever since before we were born. For example, a kick from the womb communicates something very special to a mother-to-be, that there is life inside her. This is a phenomenon familiar to all cultures.

The Mechanics

As we mentioned earlier we all communicate both with ourselves and with each other. Whilst we seem to have an inherent ability to communicate, do we really know how we do it?

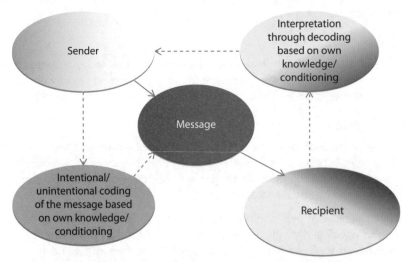

Coding and decoding is based on Age, Disability, Gender reassignment, Marriage, Maternity, Race, Religion, Sex, Sexual Orientation, social class, place of birth, occupation, and a variety of other factors.

Diagram 17

It is a little bit like the fact that many adults in the UK know how to drive a car, but first had to take driving lessons. Lessons in communication are often learnt so early in life that it can be forgotten how our communication can be received by others. To go back to our car analogy, UK visitors to Florida, and Orlando in particular, will see road signs saying they are going the wrong way; The Orlando authorities, in recognising the large proportion of visitors from the UK, realised a need to make clear the rules for driving in Orlando.

In the light of this, take a look at Diagram 17. If you follow this diagram from the top left hand corner in a straight line to the bottom right hand corner, the process of communication seems quite straightforward; we have a sender, a message and a receiver of that message. However, there are times when the message is not understood by the recipient in the way it was intended by the sender. This is particularly well explained in a now well-known book, *Men are from Mars, Women are from Venus*[34] where the author considers how communication between men and women is interpreted in different ways. Now, if we take that a step further, imagine what that may mean with communication across different communities? This is where, in our diagram above, we have the dotted line to the coding boxes. Further, it goes much deeper than just verbal communication. For example, in the UK, if a man and a woman are walking down the street holding hands, it is not seen to be anything unusual, but if the same situation involved two men it could often cause heads to turn. However in many parts of the Middle East, Africa and South Asia it is very acceptable for two men to be walking down the street holding hands, and with no presumption about their sexuality. Communication can become confounded because of the emotional underlay that is involved with each communication. An interesting example of this was given in the movie East is East, where a character whose heritage is Pakistani and for whom a marriage is arranged is talking to his friend and says, "I am not marrying an F*****g Paki." This is often a predicament that second generation migrants find themselves in; they are caught between identification with their historical roots and their adoptive culture. When a person from a given culture is displaced into a different cultural setting, it does not mean that their unconscious communication pathways are likely to change drastically.

For example, in a workplace context, we have witnessed how companies setting up call centres in South Asia and the Far East were at pains to train staff in the ways of the country they were servicing, often also insisting that the call centre representatives adopted western names. However, underlying coding and conditioning on the part of the local staff was very difficult to erase and this contributed to a sense of alienation and resentment on the part of the Western customer base. Typical complaints were, "they speak too fast," "they don't understand what I am saying," and "they have an English name but are clearly not from the UK." If we relate this to our diagram above, it becomes very apparent that communication involves not just the spoken or written word, but rather is a tapestry woven from the fibres of who we are, which includes our place of birth, heritage, gender, age, (dis)ability, social class, education and other factors.

In his book, *The Seven Habits of Highly Successful People*, the late Stephen Covey, an inspirational speaker and renowned author, incorporated the following Frank Koch story from *Proceedings*, the magazine of the U.S. Naval Institute:

> Two battleships assigned to the training squadron had been at sea on manoeuvres in heavy weather for several days. I was serving on the lead battleship and was on watch on the bridge as night fell.

> The visibility was poor with patchy fog, so the captain remained on the bridge keeping an eye on all the activities. Shortly after dark, the lookout on the wing of the bridge reported, "Light, bearing on the starboard bow." "Is it steady or is it moving astern?" the captain called out. Lookout replied, "Steady, captain," which meant we were on a dangerous collision course with that ship.

The captain then called to the signalman, "Signal that ship: We are on a collision course, advise you change your course 20 degrees."

Back came a signal, "Advisable for you to change course 20 degrees." The captain said, "Send, I'm a captain, change course 20 degrees."

"I'm a seaman second class," came the reply. "You had better change course 20 degrees." By that time, the captain was furious. He spat out, "Send, I'm a battleship. Change course 20 degrees." Back came the flashing light, "I'm a lighthouse."

Can you think of a time when you felt you were misunderstood? Take a few moments to jot down on a piece of paper the situation. As you were reviewing the situation what steps do you think you could have taken to avoid or minimise such misunderstanding?

In the case of the lighthouse story, a vital piece of information changed the whole frame of reference. In Diagram 17, we could almost view the coding and decoding mechanisms as being the vital piece of information required to create common understanding between sender and recipient. How might you be able to apply this in your organisation with your colleagues and customers?

Why is Communication so Important?

Knowing your own prejudices and biases (i.e. coding mechanisms) has often proven to be an effective route to successful communication. What better way to avoid misunderstanding than knowing where it is likely to show up? This applies on both an individual and organisational level. *Unconscious bias* can often permeate the ethos of an organisation, rather like the lingering smell of stale tobacco smoke which often is not noticed by those who have been subject to it on a long term basis. However it's immediately recognisable by someone new coming in who is a non-smoker or an ex-smoker. So, for example, when a women is appointed to a board of directors and previously there were no women on the board she is likely to pick up on the genderisation of language much more readily than her new colleagues.

In understanding the mechanics of the process depicted in Diagram 17, we can often prevent our communications from being misinterpreted. However, understanding the mechanism may also prove to be a double-edged sword when considered, for example, as per the two newspaper headlines given in Chapter six[35], Educate or Legislate.

This is a very poignant example of how the Media can, and very often do, influence thinking and embed coding into individuals and communities through persistent exposure. From a young age, people are taught to keep up with current affairs by keeping abreast of the news. Most homes today in the so called developed world have access to at least one television set and have access to the World Wide Web through computers and smartphones, tablets... usually from an early age. Prior to this status quo, children were subject to much more insular environments that embedded conditioning through primary carers who controlled the amount of external input into such conditioning. This is also reflected through the way language is used in different localities across a given country, group of countries and even continents. Taking a local example, it is quite easy to identify individuals who have been born and brought up in Newcastle, Glasgow, Liverpool, Cardiff, Birmingham and East London simply by their accents.

In the USA, it seems to be reasonably easy to distinguish folk from the Southern and Northern states. If we go to the sub-continent of India, this type of distinction can be identified even within a given state. We can see differences in styles of communication not just across cultures but even across generations and gender. Consider your own place of work and how such differences can affect communication. Even your appearance is a statement of communication that can be interpreted in a range of ways based on your own coding or hard wiring. For example, at an NHS hospital, a consultant asked one of the nurses to call Mrs. Patel, as he needed to discuss something with her that he had forgotten to mention. The nurse went to the ward and looked around but failed to find Mrs. Patel and reported back the same to the Consultant. The Consultant was a bit perplexed as he had spoken with Mrs. Patel just minutes earlier. The nurse therefore went back and asked the patients in the ward if anybody had seen Mrs. Patel. Imagine her surprise when Mrs. Patel announced herself in the bed right next to where the nurse was standing. The nurse's coding had expected Mrs. Patel to be Asian, whereas in this case, she was actually a white British born woman. Our example did not and does not make the nurse a bad person but it does highlight how misunderstanding can arise owing to our own previous conditioning.

Similarly, it is often very easy for someone to assume that another is stupid simply because they may have a speech impediment, or that another is gay because of the way they speak and/or walk, or because of the way they choose to dress. How often have you found yourself finishing someone's sentence for them? Someone with a speech impediment may well find this far more frustrating than someone without a disability. This is probably because the disabled person has encountered it far more frequently. If you consider the stereotype of the dumb blonde, it has probably caused countless frustration for such women.

Underlying beliefs and values often manifest when people find themselves in high stress situations and also when they are extremely relaxed/comfortable. In both cases, it is as if a barrier has been lifted that reveals an otherwise hidden or unconscious bias. This was witnessed in April 2011 during the UK's *Prime Minister's Question Time*, when the then Prime Minister, David Cameron, was witnessed telling a female member of the opposition to "calm down, dear." Some many months later, when he was questioned about this, the Prime Minister stated publicly that he deeply regretted what he had said. However, in the immediate aftermath of the comment, the Prime Minister chose to defend that comment and expressed an opinion when he told Grazia magazine:

> *"Samantha [Cameron's wife] does feel quite strongly about it because she often says 'calm down, dear' to me. We've both seen the commercial.*
>
> *"So while I was kicking myself, she [Samantha] didn't really see the issue."*
>
> *He also expresses Samantha's views on his calling MP Nadine Dorries "extremely frustrated" during a later Prime Minister's Questions, admitting he felt "embarrassed" ....*
>
> *Cameron blamed the 'goofs' on the heated atmosphere in the House of Commons."*[36]

So, whilst a tactic often is to try and justify what has been said or done, unconscious bias has an uncanny ability to manifest in our communications (especially when we find ourselves in stressful situations) and was reflected in David Cameron's original comments to, not one, but two women in UK Parliament. In October 2011, a similar issue erupted on a football pitch when complaints were received about comments allegedly made. The Sun Newspaper reported it in the following way:

> "ENGLAND captain John Terry is to be quizzed by cops over an alleged racist outburst at fellow soccer star Anton Ferdinand.
>
> Chelsea defender Terry, 30, could be charged with racial harassment.
>
> It carries a penalty of up to seven years' jail.
>
> Police are launching a full criminal inquiry after detectives examined video taken at a Premier League game between London sides Chelsea and Ferdinand's club Queens Park Rangers on Sunday October 23.

Terry will be interviewed under caution over allegations he called Ferdinand, left, a "f****** black ****".

No decision has been made on whether to arrest Terry.

Ferdinand, the 26-year-old younger brother of Manchester United star and ex-England captain Rio Ferdinand, will also be interviewed as a witness.

Mr Terry, at the time of writing this book, is reported to have defended himself in the following way:

Terry described the incident as a "misunderstanding" and claimed that his accusers "have leapt to the wrong conclusions about the context of what I was seen to be saying".

He added: "I would never say such a thing - and I'm saddened that people would think so."[37]

Another very common defence against allegations of sexism, racism, or any 'ism' for that matter is that the alleged aggressor will cite that they have friends from such backgrounds so that must be proof that they are not being discriminatory. One of the authors experienced a situation when he was 8 years old where he was with his friends and they decided that they were going to go "Paki bashing." In this context, such activity was targeted at anybody who looked Indian, like the author, or Pakistani. He was expected to join in and even questioned, hesitantly, about this. He was told, "It's ok, you're one of us!"

Ralph Waldo Emerson[38] stated it in the following way:

"Who you are speaks so loudly I can't hear what you're saying."

Experience shows us that, as mentioned earlier, we tend to revert to our core conditioning (see chapter 1, Identity and Culture) when we are in highly stressful situations. For some people it reveals unconscious prejudices and biases that have no logical substance. How often, especially in an economic downturn, do we hear about migrants *coming over and taking over our jobs*? A similar situation was experienced by Jewish refugees settling in the East End of London in the pre- and post-Second World War eras. Interestingly, this pattern seems to play out more and more frequently; we have seen similar attitudes towards Eastern Europeans in the UK in recent times. Core tribal behaviours manifest when we feel under threat and, therefore, unconsciously revert to type.

When considering communication either within a community or across communities it is often useful to understand what tone and non-verbal factors are likely to mean. For example, when a car horn is used, it communicates different things in different parts of the world. In the UK, the sounding of a car horn officially means you are making someone aware of your presence, but how often is it used in that way? In many parts of Asia and the Middle East, it is used as a means to announce your presence and to caution other drivers not to get in the way. In the UK, honking the horn often signifies annoyance and frustration.

More locally, and in your own workplace, when a line manager is giving feedback to a staff member, how much consideration is given to how to communicate, especially when it may be a performance and conduct issue? There was a study done at a major hospital in the UK where it was found that the rates of disciplinary proceedings amongst black and minority ethnic (BME) staff were much higher than with white staff. Further investigation revealed that this situation arose because line managers who were mainly white were often very anxious about being branded as being racist when it came to managing the performance of their BME staff. As a result they were far more likely to adopt formal procedures in managing BME staff performance by comparison to the white staff that they managed.

Chapter 5

The Customer is Always Right!?

The latest news headlines reported how Mavis, a middle-aged woman, was mugged in broad daylight by youths wielding a baseball bat. She received 48 stitches and was black and blue through bruising, but the good news? She made a full recovery. One day, on approaching the Customer Services Representative at her local bank, she asked to be served by someone else. The Customer Services Representative explained that he was fully able to deal with Mavis' banking requirements, whereupon Mavis asked to see the manager and demanded that she be served by a white cashier...

Is it appropriate to accede to every customer demand? In the situation given above, the customer was worth an estimated £125,000 a year to the bank and had been attacked by someone who appeared to be from an African-Caribbean background. What should the manager have done and how would such a decision affect the business as a whole? If the manager agrees to finding an alternative white person to serve the customer, it will preserve the customer relationship but will serve to discriminate against the Black Customer Service Representative who has been a valued member of staff and is equally competent to handle the customer's requirements. As much as we may have sympathy for Mavis and her situation, would she have insisted on being served by a black person if her attacker had been white? This is a very good example of Direct Discrimination and why it is illegal in UK law. The situation described, actually did happen in a UK Bank and, quite rightly, the Manager made the appropriate judgement call.

The foundation of most businesses is based on a combination of value for money and excellent service. The balance between the two will be determined by the organisations' strategic positioning, which may mean a philosophy of 'pile it high, sell it cheap' or providing a customised product/service for a potentially much higher price. The UK Press reported David Beckham's famous hair cut that cost what some would consider to be an abnormal sum of money. Some would argue that an average barber would have done as good a job at a fraction of the price. This is not a problem as long as it is not discriminatory. For example, the hairdresser serving David Beckham may well be happy to serve anyone as long as they are willing to pay the same price, regardless of race, colour, creed, disability, age, etc....

Business, however, for us, is not a term reserved just for the private sector but relates to employment and service provision in the public, education and not for profit sectors, too.

The lifeblood of any business can be said to be its customers or service users; without them, there would not be a need for such a business or organisation. For example with the introduction of student fees the higher education sector has little choice but to think of its students as paying customers. In reality a number of Universities had already picked up on this theme and had started a drive towards attracting international students, particularly from South East Asia.

In today's marketplace, organisations cannot ignore the impact of globalisation and local demographics if they wish to be successful. A classic example of this was the *World's Local*

Bank advertising campaign launched by HSBC in the late 1990s. It allowed a diverse customer base to connect with their roots and provided valuable information to other customers about local customs and traditions, creating a sense of common appreciation. In the longer term, this secured a broader, more diverse, customer base and hence increased business opportunities for the bank.

How then, can we reconcile a situation where, in today's increasingly global marketplace, organisations practice target marketing which appears to discriminate against certain groups of people? Some would argue that target marketing itself is discriminatory because it excludes some proportion of the customer base. There is a difference between target marketing and exclusion (which can sometimes be very deliberate).

Who is the Customer?

The customer could be anybody who wishes to buy our products and services. For example, the Fire Service provides a service to all people within their catchment area but the individual customer pays for it indirectly (e.g. through taxes) Thus, sometimes the individual is a customer by choice (e.g. I wish to buy my groceries from the local store) and at other times by circumstance (e.g. the council will contract someone to collect my refuse and I do not have a say in the appointment of the collector). Whomsoever our customers are, we need to maximise the benefits our organisations bring to them if we are to continue being successful.

Where we are providing a service, it can often be that we only provide that service in a manner that we have always provided it. If that is not in line with changing needs and demographics, we may be reducing the prospect of profitability or not utilising resources efficiently. Especially in an economic downturn, this could have quite serious impacts in terms of on-going business sustainability and profitability.

For example, in Public Healthcare, services are provided to a diverse customer base, Where needs are not met, not only will certain service users end up feeling marginalised, the organisation will also not be making best use of public funds. When spending cuts are the order of the day, it becomes much more important to provide services in a manner that will make them accessible to all those requiring them. In this way we would get maximum value from scarce funding.

In order to ensure that the organisation is maximising its service capability it is necessary to ensure that strategic direction takes account of the needs of a diverse customer base and then integrates properly into operations and service delivery. However, human nature is such that it feels easier just to do what was always done (imprinting, explained in Chapter 1). Which option carries the bigger risk? In our opinion, there is not one right answer, but rather a need to review and modify as required. This is where the idea of Equality Impact Analysis (now commonly referred to as Equality Assessment, UK Law) can bring significant value to our customer bases and our workforces.

Many organisations now recognise that their workforce needs to reflect their customer base if they are to remain effective and competitive. Of necessity, this requires a comprehensive recognition and understanding of the variety of skills, qualities and cultures required to keep our businesses profitable and our services effective.

If we consider UK demographics, we can see that there is a rising trend of people living longer and fewer people being born. This in itself poses a new set of challenges, to ensure the viability and ongoing sustainability of our businesses to cater for the needs of an aging population[39]

With the onset of age there is an increasing experience of disability, for example, the deterioration of vision and the greater incidence of hearing impairment. Additionally we are aware of other conditions such as Dementia, Parkinson's and Alzheimer's which carry other impediments for customers. The spending power of disabled people, as far back as 2004, was estimated at £80 billion per annum by the then UK Government's Department for Work and Pensions. Other research conducted by the charity Scope and reported by the Business Disability Forum in March 2015 showed that, "Drawing upon research conducted by Business Disability Forum (BDF) in 2006 on the value of the 'Walk Away Pound', or the income lost by businesses that fail to make goods and services accessible to disabled people, the Commission surveyed over 2000 disabled people to find that businesses are losing an estimated £1.8 billion a month by ignoring the needs of disabled customers."[40]

Far from seeing the needs of a diverse customer base as an avoidable cost businesses need to recognise the investment in terms of future returns. For example, in the case of disabled customers, physical adjustments to premises will often be one-time costs that will benefit countless employees and customers alike. Furthermore, governmental support schemes, such as 'Access to Work', provide financial assistance to employers who need to make reasonable adjustments for their workers. Other adjustments would likely be offset against taxes.

Making some basic mistakes can cost a huge amount of money which could have been avoided by some useful diversity related market research and effective Equality Analysis.

Organisations failing to make this investment also need to consider the much broader reputational risk pursuant to ignoring the diversity present in the customer base. For example, Clarke's Shoes being branded with Hindu Deities saw an extreme reaction across the Hindu community globally; Row over naming shoes after Hindu Gods.

> "Britain's Hindu community is up in arms against one of the country's largest shoemakers, Clarks, for naming two new designs of shoes after the deities Vishnu and Krishna.
>
> The names appear on the boxes in which they are supplied and not on the shoes themselves. The Vishnu shoe is a £30 summer sandal in metallic, black or navy blue, while the Krishna is a black boot retailing at £89. The trouble first started when someone in Leicester bought the sandal… and noticed the name on the box. Community leaders [said] they complained to Clarks, which refused to withdraw the sandal. They [said they went public because the company has now introduced the winter boot, Krishna, into the market.]
>
> Clarks has apologised and ordered its staff to cover up the names on the shoeboxes. A spokesman for the company, John Keery, said, "The names were picked in all innocence and only used internally for the staff to identify different styles of shoes easily. They were not meant to offend anyone." Keery said that the complaints had come from Hindu organisations rather than from customers, but they were concerned to not cause any offence.
>
> Mahesh Prasher, secretary of the Hindu Religious and Cultural Society in Leicester said that Hindus could not have been more insulted. "Footwear is considered unclean in our religion," he explained, "and that is why shoes are always removed before entering temples. Hindus also consider the cow to be sacred, so to associate both footwear and leather products with our gods causes huge offence and insult."
>
> Others who claim and aspire to be 'community leaders' have added their voices to the clamour. The recently ennobled Lord Bagri, chairman of the London Metal Exchange, says that he is "disappointed and concerned at the lack of research by the company. In a multi-racial and multi-religious society like we have in this country, it is the obligation of marketing departments to make sure that they do not cause offence to religious and other sensitivities."
>
> Keith Vaz, Labour MP for Leicester and self-styled spokesman for all ethnic causes, explained:
>
> "you are not supposed to call the things you walk on after gods. The Christian equivalent would be to name a line of shoes after Jesus and the Virgin Mary. I am very concerned

and have written to Clarks for an explanation. I don't want to go over the top, but there are religious points that need looking into."

A spokesperson for Britain's largest Hindu temple, the Swaminarayan temple in London, which takes pains to present Hinduism as a modern rational religion, struck a different note:

"I am sure it was not mean to be disrespectful. Mistakes happen and it is a part of human life. The fact that products are named after gods does not affect the status of the gods. "Clarks is the second shoe company to find itself in difficulties with the men of god".

The sports goods manufacturer, Nike, was criticised for using a symbol of Allah on a range of training shoes, and India's former cricket captain, Mohammad Azharuddin, found himself in trouble with a section of Muslims for autographing a range of Reebok shoes, since he not only associated the name of the prophet with the shoe, but actually inscribed it on the shoe.

The ever vigilant Hindus of Leicester have, in the past, protested against other businesses who appear to be showing disrespect to their gods. In 1992, they demanded that a French waste management company remove its initials, SITA, from the sides of its garbage vans, as this is the name of a Hindu goddess."

Copyright © 1997, Indian Express Newspapers (Bombay) Ltd.

http://www.expressindia.com/ie/daily/19971107/31150713.html

A similar article appeared in the US press:

'Hindu' Shoes Withdrawn after Protests ▬▬▬▬

Source: http://www.rediff.com/us/2000/aug/01us.htm

Indians in the United States rallied together to oppose shoe designs offensive to religious sentiments, reports on Tuesday said.

The high-heeled sandals with colourful portrayals of Hindu deities were marketed by a California-based company and manufactured in China.

The sandals, sold at five dollars a pair, were withdrawn from the market soon after Indian-American Hindu leaders protested, according to a New York ethnic paper News India. The sandals with psychedelic designs bore the images of deities like Shiva, Ganesha and Parvati.

In a letter to the association, Patrick Huang, the attorney of the shoe company Fortune Dynamic Inc, regretted the manufacture of the footwear. He said the manufacture of the sandals had been discontinued and that the company did not intend to disparage the Hindu religion or offend those practising the religion.

The American Hindus Against Defamation, a coalition of major Hindu organisations in North America, had expressed outrage at the introduction of the shoes and demanded an apology for this "inconsiderate" act, according to the Asian Age newspaper. Others termed it "horrendous, incredible and thoroughly offensive".

This is not the first time that shoe designs have offended sensibilities. Three years ago, footwear giant Nike faced a lot of flak for using the symbol Allah on a new range of training shoes. A shop in Leicester, England, selling shoes embroidered with quotations from the Koran, was set on fire.

If we go back further in history, the 1970's and 80's saw a wide scale boycott of Barclays Bank because of its reported links to the Apartheid regime of South Africa.

It is not only one business that might be impacted, especially when we consider multinational and national organisations, the domino effect means that there is a dependency that feeds back all the way down the supply chain with each supplier having its own customers. Additionally organisations will have both internal and external customers. Front-line staff, who are the face of the organisation to external customers, often are dependent on back-office and support functions (internal customers) to do their job effectively.

Customer-focused versus Sales- (Target-) Driven

Understanding our customers and their needs has proven to be a very effective route to repeat business. Leading business gurus tell us that it would cost us far more to attract new customers than to gain repeat business from existing customers. Target marketing is also much more effective once an organisation understands its customer base. For example, Tesco Clubcard members may well receive promotional vouchers for products outside of their normal purchasing habits but still related to their lifestyle.

However, this practice can sometimes backfire when a customer is provided with promotions for, for example, meat products when all of the customer's shopping history shows that they are vegetarian; this is more a case of being sales driven than customer focused. Conversely, when planned effectively, target marketing can be beneficial. For example a supermarket located in an area largely inhabited by the Orthodox Hasidic (Jewish) community decided to close at sunset on a Friday and to re-open at sunset on a Saturday. They were thereby able to stay open on a Sunday when other stores had to close after 6 hours of trading. Which gave them an advantage on their competitors.

Customer focus can often be lost when we are not aware of the stereotypical biases that we may be holding unconsciously. For example, a situation occurred in which a sales rep lost a deal because he was sales driven rather than customer focused. The case in question concerned a car showroom where the sales representative talked over, and systematically ignored, the questions posed by the customer as he gave all his attention to her male partner.

When considering customer focus and access to products and services for disabled people, there is a perception (perhaps created by the use of a wheelchair as a universal symbol for disability) that accessibility is about ramps and level access. Organisations also need to consider the broader aspects of access for their employees and customers/service users. For example, a letter from a Financial Services organisation informed the reader, at the bottom of the letter, that the communication was also available in Braille or other formats. This is excellent as long as the reader mentions it to those who require such alternative formats. With modern day technology (e.g. as seen in talking greetings cards), it will likely become economically viable for an audio message 'chip' to be inserted into this type of letter in the future. Upon opening the letter, the recipient would receive the message in a format that allows him or her to access the crucial information about the alternative format.

Customer Channels

With the globalisation of workforces and customer bases, access to goods and services has increased significantly from just physical channels to more virtual marketplaces, including telecoms, computers, mobile devices, etc. For example, Bluetooth messaging when you are in the vicinity of a store is now becoming an accepted part of the marketing mix. Equally, such technology can be used to attract potential employees who may not otherwise have an awareness of the different opportunities available with given employers.

Gone are the days when people just went out shopping or relied on a physical intermediary (such as a personal insurance broker). Co-operative insurance services, for example, used to offer a door-to-door insurance premium collection service, and Barrs used to sell bottled soft drinks in a similar way. The difference now is that people can still receive home deliveries but choose to order online. Different delivery channels will suit different customers at different times. Organisations therefore benefit from providing a range of shopping options which will meet the needs of the broadest range of customers.

During the month of Ramadan, Muslim customers may prefer to do a lot more of their shopping online rather than having to buy it from stores where they are exposed to food and drink items which are prohibited during daylight hours. Such an option was not available before the start of this millennium. Banking is now available 24/7 for the majority of customers, enabling those who may, for example, observe a Sabbath on certain days of the week to still have access to their banking facilities outside of conventional times. Aside from meeting the needs of a specific customer segment, the variety of channels gives all customers greater access to the goods and services provided by the respective organisation.

Hotels in the UK, Europe and the USA now routinely offer as standard accessible rooms for people with disabilities, which very often are situated on the ground level. This is becoming the norm, whereas once it was seen as a great inconvenience by hoteliers. When such organisations are providing a service to the public in the UK, case law has established that the owners or proprietors/management may not discriminate against people with particular protected characteristics[41] even when it may appear to be offensive to someone with another protected characteristic (for example, in this case Christian beliefs versus sexual orientation).

We have also seen examples of where market segmentation strategies have backfired. Earlier we recounted the Clark's Shoes situation which was not a conscious attempt to offend anybody. Another very good example of this was an advertising campaign run by MacDonald's, featuring US sign-language users, which led to a unprecedented number of sign-language users arriving at MacDonald's and the staff not being able to cope because they had not received any instruction in sign language. MacDonalds however choose to respond positively and took a decision to proactively train staff in US sign language at that time.

With the emergence of what has been termed the Global Village, organisations are recognising the value of a diverse customer base as a key component of the business/marketing mix. From our own experience, whilst many organisations state that they value a diverse and inclusive workforce, this has not yet translated into sufficient proportionality across all levels of the respective organisations.

Reputation and Risk

People go into business with the intention of creating economic success. The same can be said of all service providers, who are looking to maximise the service provided within a given budget. In the UK, following the recession, in the wake of the global banking crisis, this factor has become ever more pronounced. Allied to this, and a trend that has been increasingly imported from the USA is the threat of litigation. In the 21st Century, The UK has become a far more litigious society than at any point in its history. This is evidenced by the volume of organisations willing to advertise their 'no win, no fee' services, particularly on daytime television.

Complaints & Conflict

UK Equality Legislation states that all customers should be able to access goods and services regardless of their Age, Disability, Gender, etc... There is often an issue in that customers can claim to be discriminated against whereas, in actuality, this may not be the case; the principle of reasonable adjustment means that alternative ways of providing the service may need to be considered for people with disabilities by way of an example. Equally, an organisation needs to understand what it needs to do to protect itself in the event that customers' actions may unlawfully discriminate against staff and/or customers.

All organisations have policies, which are not always published to the world at large, and can be referred to for guidance by members of the workforce. Some policies are clearly given a lot more prominence than others, for example, Health and Safety. Here it is interesting to note that Equality carries the underpinning of Health and Safety. When an individual does not feel safe in the workplace owing to one or more aspects of their difference, then this is a health and safety issue as much as it is an Equality and Inclusion issue. A very good example of this is where a person is being bullied or harassed. There was a real life situation where two people walked into a Pub in London and, unknown to them was a favourite haunt of people from the Republic of Ireland. Three minutes after they walked in they were met with a statement of "up the Irish." This created a very intimidating situation and the 'new' customers felt they had no choice but to leave as they feared for their own safety. This could have been any other community, but the point was that the new customers felt vulnerable and threatened to an extent where they left the Pub. It asks a question about the obligation of the Publican towards those two customers. It could be argued that the Publican sided with the 'regular' customers to protect their business. However, it is known that dissatisfied customers are far more likely to tell friends and family about bad customer experiences rather than good customer service. What might the consequences then be if this was, say, a well-known chain of pubs?

Against such a culture of passive acceptance, it is important to make prevention, rather than cure, the better option, through the establishment, for example, of a Customer Charter that sets out in clear and unequivocal language what customers can expect from their suppliers; we consider the Open University's student charter to be a good example.[42] This is because it is explicit enough to make it understandable, and within context, without being too complex. A Charter should also detail how to seek recourse in the event of a complaint. This is an area in which many internet-based companies do fail their customers. For example, if you were to select a large supplier website at random and wished to find someone to actually speak to, the search could take anywhere from 5 to 30 minutes (or longer), and even then you might not succeed.

In a culture where shareholder returns are often uppermost in the minds of Boards of Directors, difficult decisions are taken to balance the cost of human interaction versus automated systems. Where can a customer go to when they feel they need to understand their rights and responsibilities? Organisations have started to adopt the idea of the customer charter…

Customer Charter

When an organisation makes a proactive commitment to placing equality and diversity at the heart of its Customer Charter it is sending a clear message, to the world it serves, about its intent. In our view, at its heart, a good Charter is easy to understand and states the business's commitment to providing the best possible service to *all* customers. Clearly, then, this includes those customers who may have been subject to disadvantage. For example, in the UK, we are seeing more and more aspects of public travel becoming accessible to people with disabilities.

What, then, should a good Customer Charter encompass? According to the Institute of Customer Services[43] it should:

> "…improve access to an organisation's services and promote quality. It does this by telling customers the standards of service to expect, what to do if something goes wrong, and how to make contact. A Customer Charter/Code of Practice helps employees too, by setting out clearly the services their organisation provides."

It goes on to state that the core components of a Charter should include the following:

- *spell out the standards of service customers can expect*
- *tell customers how to complain if something goes wrong, or service is not met, or how to offer a suggestion for improvement*
- *make clear how customers can contact an organisation and get further information*
- *make sure the information is accessible and easy to understand*
- *fully involve customers and employees in its preparation*
- *explain how an organisation is planning for further improvement*
- *assure customers that they will receive a fair service*
- *say if there is any relevant legislation*
- *make sure that the publication date is clearly visible, and ensure the content remains current*

When we consider the issues of Diversity and Inclusion, then these elements are very clear in that they are about *all* customers not just the majority of customers. For example, if we were to take, "make sure the information is accessible and easy to understand," this would need to accommodate those customers who have learning disabilities and/or other varying needs such as text phone or language challenges. In the case of the first bullet point above, "*tell customers how to complain if something goes wrong, or service is not met, or how to offer a suggestion for improvement.*" , if an organisation is unclear about how to improve its service to those customers/service users from historically disadvantaged groups, then the Charter is an excellent medium for inviting feedback to help the Organisation make its products/services more accessible. Greater use of the products and services increases the sustainability of the business/service.

An example of a good Customer Charter that we found on the Internet was Nat West Bank[44] because it is clear and concise, using plain language that most people would understand.

Chapter 6

Educate or Legislate

The interview went really well and I was ecstatic to be told that I had been offered the job. I accepted on the phone and told John, my boss to be, that I was really looking forward to this opportunity especially as my partner and I were looking to settle down and start a family; working in a growing organisation with good prospects was just the icing on the cake. Imagine my shock when I received an email telling me that, owing to an administrative error, they had mistakenly made the offer and that they would not be going ahead with my appointment. Apparently someone else had performed better than me!

What could be the logical assumption in the above case? If you had to make a guess, would you say that the candidate was male or female? Why? Once upon a time, this would have been covered under the Sex Discrimination Act, but since the passing to the Equality Act 2010, it might be covered under the Protected Characteristic of *Pregnancy and Maternity* and/ or subsequent regulations on *Shared Parental Leave*.

As we discussed in chapter 1, attitudes tend to manifest in behaviour. When discrimination takes place, it is because the individuals concerned are working against a constant bombardment of negativity based on historical prejudice (learned behaviour) that is reinforced through the mass media; individual issues are thus generalised to whole communities and populations. The result: unconscious or, sometimes, very deliberate bias in the way people from minority groups can be treated both at work and in the community. Examples of this have been evident during the last century or so, and continue in the present day. The headlines below, for example, appeared in two national UK newspapers on 17th June 2011.

School's ban on boy's cornrows is 'indirect racial discrimination'

High court rules against London secondary school after boy was refused entry for breaching ban on 'gang-related' hairstyles

Ban on 'gang culture' haircuts in school is 'indirect racial discrimination', judge rules

A London school's decision to ban hairstyles it says have become associated with gang culture has resulted in "unlawful, indirect racial discrimination which is not justified," a court has ruled.[45]

One of these headlines clearly depict an intention to provoke a reaction based on generations of nurtured stereotypical perspectives.

How, then, do we address the core of the real issues at play, to support the principal of socio-diversity? Is the answer just to allow Nature to take its course? In the absence of effective education around the principles and practices of equality, diversity and inclusion, what might be the consequences? The following is an extract from Harriet Harman's (the then UK Government

Minister for Women and Equality) Ministerial *Introduction to the consultation on consolidation of Equality Legislation*[46] in the UK, July 2008:

Time to strengthen the law

While a combination of laws and wider action has brought us a long way over the past 40 years, inequality and discrimination persist today.

Even in the 21st century, and in one of the most dynamic economies in the world, achieving greater equality is still an issue.

The gender pay gap, though down from 17.4% in 1997, still means that a woman's full time pay is on average 12.6% less per hour than a man's. Women working part-time are paid around 40% less per hour;

The rate of employment of disabled people has risen from 38% ten years ago to 48% today, but if you are disabled, you are still two and a half times more likely to be out of work than a non-disabled person;

If you are from an ethnic minority, in 1997 you were 17.9% less likely to find work than if you are white. The difference is still 15.5%;

62% of over-fifties feel that they are turned down for a job because they are considered too old, compared with 5% of people In their thirties;

6 out of 10 lesbian and gay schoolchildren experience homophobic bullying and half of those contemplate killing themselves as a result.

Unless we step up progress:

The pay gap between men and women will not close until 2085

It will take almost 100 years for people from ethnic minorities to get the same job prospects as white people;

Disabled people will probably never get the same job prospects;

It will take 20 years for women to achieve equal representation in the Senior Civil Service; and

It will take 80 years to elect a representative House of Commons.

In 2010/2011, the debate was then diverted to a question of fairness. Here below is an extract of Theresa May, the then Home Secretary's speech on 17th November 2010:

...no government should try to ensure equal outcomes for everyone.

But we do need to recognise that in trying to ensure equality of opportunity – the "gap" still matters.

Those growing up in households which have fallen too far behind have fewer opportunities available to them and they are less able to take the opportunities that are available. We see it with families of three generations who have no qualifications and no job.

But you do not improve the lives of those at the bottom by limiting the ambitions and opportunities of others. Instead, we need to design intelligent policies that give those at the bottom real opportunities to make a better life for themselves.

Achieving equality of treatment and equality of opportunity are aims that the vast majority of people would regard as sensible and noble goals for government policy.

But in recent years, equality has become a dirty word because it meant something different. It came to be associated with the worst forms of pointless political correctness and social engineering.

I want to turn around the equalities agenda and I want to change people's perception of what the government is trying to achieve on equality.

I want us to move away from the identity politics of the past – where government thought it knew all about you because you ticked a box on a form or fitted into a certain category – and instead start to recognise that we are a nation of 62 million individuals. And that means demonstrating that equality is for everyone by making it a part of everyday life.

And I want us to move away from the arrogant notion from government that it knows best. Government can act as a leader, a convenor and an advocate for change. But on its own it will only ever make limited progress. We need to work with people, communities and businesses to empower them to enact change.

Only if we do that; only if we work with the grain of human nature, not against it, will we achieve the fairer, more equal and more prosperous society that we all want to see.

Where a democratic government is elected by the people for the people and to represent the people, what role should it assume in order to ensure fairness? Today, there are probably more people in prisons in the UK since at any other time in UK history. Surely it is the government that must decide how best to handle/minimise crime through prevention and enforcement by the police service, whereas the judiciary can set appropriate penalties for criminals. Discrimination is a criminal act, not a civil act. We contend, therefore, that it falls to government to put appropriate steps in place to handle/minimise and ultimately eradicate discrimination and unfairness in terms of the workplace and the provision of goods and services. The Equality Act 2010 took significant steps towards such an aim.

The intention behind Equalities legislation in the UK has never been about organising quotas but much more about creating an environment that allows each individual to reach their full potential. Whilst this chapter considers legislation, our intention is to think about the spirit of the legislation rather than the letter of the law. There are many legal websites which will provide comprehensive information about the technical aspects of UK equality law.

Protected Characteristics

Protected Characteristic is a phrase coined under the Equality Act 2010 to identify communities of people who have historically faced discrimination and disadvantage. We would only need to look at semi-biographical novels such as 'The Naked Civil Servant' to get a perspective on the type of treatment received. In UK Law there are 9 such Protected Characteristics:

- Age
- Disability
- Gender Reassignment
- Marriage and Civil Partnership
- Pregnancy and Maternity
- Race
- Religion or Belief
- Sex (previously referred to as 'Gender', but amended to distinguish from Gender Reassignment)
- Sexual Orientation

Age

Typically when someone thinks about Age their thoughts go to people who are much older than them.

UK Law protects anyone of a particular age (e.g. 32-year-olds) or a range of ages (e.g. 18–30-year-olds). It is unlawful to discriminate against someone because they are a certain age unless there are exceptions in Law. For example it is unlawful for someone under the age of 17 to drive a car on public roads in the UK. This is clearly discriminatory for people under 17 but falls within the remit of the Law.

The terms young and old cannot be seen as absolutes but rather as relative. For example 17 years of age could be seen as an absolute. Whether this person of 17 is young or old is relative to the age of the person who is considering them. Typically, people think of young as under 25, but a 30 year old would not see themselves as old. However, in the past employers may have discounted a 30 year old as being too young for a senior executive position.

Similarly at the other end of the spectrum UK Law was changed to abolish the then long standing mandatory retirement age. Employers now cannot force someone to retire as a set age. As a result this can pose a dilemma for employers as to when it is appropriate to insist that a worker takes retirement. As long as the decision can be objectively justified and presented in an appropriate manner to the employee, then in our opinion this would be seen as a fair approach. By way of a parallel example, individuals may be required to retake their driving test each year once they pass the age of 75.

Something to consider

In a restructuring situation all people aged 60 and over are offered voluntary redundancy. Samuel complained to his manager because he felt that he should be entitled to apply for voluntary redundancy, too. His manager did not take him seriously and asked him why he wanted to be like the old fogies.

Does Samuel have a valid complain?

Our response

Since the introduction of age as a protected characteristic it would be unlawful for an organisation to offer voluntary redundancy only to people in a certain age bracket unless it is for reasons of objective justification.

In this case, if the organisation could demonstrate that the only way they would be able to create a more age diversity across the whole organisation was by offering voluntary redundancy to people within the older age bracket, it could be objectively justified.

Disability

Under UK Law protection is provided to anyone with a physical or mental impairment that has a substantial adverse impact, is long-term (likely to last 12 months or longer) and has an adverse effect on their ability to carry out normal day-to-day activities.

Disability is frequently described in terms of a Social model and a Medical model. In a nut shell, the Medical model seeks to describe a person's condition. The Social model says that society presents barriers for a disabled person regardless of their ability. For example under the medical model a person with severe diabetes can function as long as they balance their insulin and their diet. Under the Social model the same person may be frowned upon for taking frequent breaks to administer medication and/or eat because they are deemed to be taking liberties that others are not afforded.

Disability does not necessarily equate to inability. Take Stephen Hawking for example, a Cambridge scholar and professor of Mathematics, who has made a significant contribution to the field of Physics.

Disabilities can be visible and invisible. For example, whilst a person without a limb is clearly recognised as having a disability, somebody with Dyslexia or Asperger Syndrome may well be regarded as being stupid or unsociable respectively; they are not recognised as having a disability until this information is revealed. The Law provides protection even where you simply think someone has a disability or where you have discriminated against someone because of their association with a disabled person.

Something to consider

Mary was very efficient in her work. This, however, did not stop colleagues from gossiping and moaning about the fact that she always seemed to be disappearing 10 minutes before lunch break. What was not noticed was that Mary usually started work 15 minutes before others, and often did not leave until 15 minutes after them. What colleagues did not know was that Mary needed to replace here Colostomy bag ever since she had had her colon removed when she was working at another company.

It was becoming apparent to the line manager that there was some disquiet amongst the team about Mary and so he sent out a general memo reminding staff that they must observe their contractual obligations regarding time keeping and punctuality.

As she was passing the staff common room Mary overheard a couple of colleagues talking about the memo saying, "It's about time he [the manager] did something about Mary skiving off every day. Mary was very upset by this comment and complained to the manager about being harassed. The manager retorted that, "Well what do you expect, Mary, your colleagues see you disappearing 10 minutes ahead of lunch break every day and I cannot condone that sort of behaviour.

What would you have done if you had been Mary's line manager?

Our response

Good practice would suggest that Mary's line manager ought to have noticed long before the issue became a talking point in the office. Then he would have been justified in asking Mary for a reason behind her needing to leave the office 10 minutes before the lunch break. This would have given Mary an opportunity to discuss her disability and come to a more formal arrangement with regards to a reasonable adjustment.

Additionally if there is an issue that is related to one specific person then it is inappropriate to send a communication to all staff about that issue; this will avoid others who are not implicated from feeling that they have been criticised for something that does not apply to them.

Gender Reassignment

Protection is afforded to someone who is, or who is in the process of, transitioning from one gender to another.

UK law has chosen to differentiate Gender from Sex. Sex is often primarily related to the physical attributes of a male or female, whereas gender refers to the emotional, cultural and social identity of a person that may or may not include the medical model of sex as being determined by which set of genitalia a person has.

This applies to all people who are planning, undergoing or have (partially) completed gender reassignment.

A transsexual ("Trans") person who, emotionally and psychologically, feels that they belong to the opposite sex and they may or may not have completely reassigned gender through surgery.

A transvestite is a man who prefers to dress in a manner that is more conventionally attributed to women. The same term does not apply to women who chose to dress in a manner more conventionally 'male'. This is because convention has accepted that Women may wear trousers and shirts but men wearing skirts and stockings is still not a socially acceptable convention.

Transvestites are not covered under gender reassignment unless their transvestism is part of a planned progression to gender reassignment

The most common concern that worries team members when they are informed that a colleague is undergoing gender reassignment is which toilet they will be using. This is particularly the case where a pre-op man is transitioning to a woman.

Something to consider

Joseph is a Born Again Christian and has been managing Chris for the last two years. Chris is an expert in his field and would not be easy to replace. One Monday morning Joseph greets Chris and says, "You wouldn't believe it but I swear I saw a women who looked just like you when I was out shopping with my wife yesterday. Chris became somewhat embarrassed and said, "Could I have a quick word with you?" Joseph agreed and they met in a meeting room 15 minutes later. Chris told Joseph in the meeting that there was no easy way to say it, but he was transitioning to female and it was her, whom Chris saw, yesterday morning. About a week later Joseph called Chris in to a meeting and informed him that the team was being restructured and it meant that Chris's role was now going to be redundant.

What might be Chris's options in this situation?

Our response

Gender reassignment is a Protected Characteristic and, as such, Chris could rightfully infer that his role being made redundant is linked directly to him revealing his Trans status to Joseph. Chris would be able to, in the first instance, invoke the company's grievance and complaints procedure if he feels that he is unable to challenge Joseph directly.

Should Chris feel he did not get a satisfactory outcome as a result of the complaint of direct discrimination on account of gender reassignment he could, after following due process, file a case at tribunal.

Marriage and Civil Partnership

Marriage is traditionally, in many religions, defined as a 'union between a man and a woman'. Since 2013, UK law recognised marriages for same-sex couples. Same sex couples can also have their relationships legally recognised as 'civil partnerships'.

Protection is afforded to anybody who is discriminated against on account of their marital or civil partnership status

An exemption granted in Law is that Churches have discretion to decide whether or not to permit a same sex marriage within their institution or constitution. There is still much controversy about the relationship between certain Protected Characteristics and which Characteristic would take priority. For example a gay cleric registered a civil partnership and this was unknown to the parish congregation. The regional bishop, received complaints from concerned parishioners asking what the church was proposing to do about the gay priest. The Church could lawfully ask the Cleric to step down from his priest duties.

Under UK Law, Religions have been given dispensation to decide whether a practising Cleric who happens to be gay is within the conscience guidelines of that Faith. However in other, employment based, situations it would not be acceptable for a person of a particular faith background to refuse to work with another married or single person whom they think is Lesbian, Gay, Bi Sexual or Transgendered. Similarly, in the example given above, had the Cleric been an administrative manager then the Occupational Requirement dispensation would not apply.

In a typical work or customer service situation the marital status of a person should be irrelevant and such an individual needs to be afforded the same opportunities and service level as anybody else. Since the introduction of same sex marriages this is even more so.

Something to consider

Miss Pringle who rents a house from the council phones to say that she is about to get married and wants a new rent book in joint names. The customer service representative is very happy for them asks "who is the lucky man?" The customer suddenly gets very irate and says "how dare you make assumptions about me."

The customer service representative is perplexed!

What do you think is the issue?

Our response

Miss Pringle was offended because it was not the first time that others had assumed she was marrying a man. The customer services representative had, unwittingly, made an assumption that Miss Pringle was about to marry a man. This could be deemed to be an easy mistake to make. However, it is important that we recognise others as being individuals and therefore it becomes even more important to base our responses only to known information.

Pregnancy and Maternity

Where pregnancy is the condition of expecting a baby, maternity refers to the period after the birth, and gives rise to maternity leave in the employment context. According to the Equality and Human Rights Commission, protection is extended to:

- A woman for 26 weeks (and up to 52 weeks) after giving birth.
- A woman who is treated unfavourably because she is breastfeeding (especially in a public place).
- A man being treated unfairly because he has to bottle feed his child.
- A man who is treated unfairly because he has elected to take a portion of his partners maternity leave because his wife/partner has chosen to return to work.

Something to consider

An employer, recruiting for a permanent post, selected and offered a job to a man. Subsequently, during the 'offer' phone call the employer learns that the 'new' employee's partner is expecting a baby and that he is really looking forward to bonding with his baby during the time he will be sharing parental leave next year. A short while later, the employer called back and retracted the job offer, saying he had made a mistake and contacted the wrong person.

Could this be direct discrimination?

Our response

Under these circumstances it would be reasonable to conclude that the offer conversation influenced the employer to retract the offer of employment. The likelihood is that a tribunal would infer that discrimination took place unless there was compelling evidence to prove the strength of the other candidate for the job.

Prior to the introduction of shared parental leave in the UK, this could have been deemed as indirect discrimination under pregnancy and maternity.

Race (Ethnicity and Nationality)

Race refers to a person's:

- Nationality
- Ethnic, regional or national origins.

While Religion is covered specifically as a separate Protected Characteristic, skin colour is often regarded as an implicit aspect of Race

It is unlawful to treat someone less favourably because of their race, colour, nationality or ethnic origins either in the workplace or in the provision of goods and services. For example, it would be inappropriate to hold a public community event in an official venue of the British National Party.

Protection in UK law extends to all people whether they are majority (i.e. white British) or minority ethnic. There are situations where the person being discriminated against is in a minority situation in spite of being white and British.

A development in UK Law in 2013 was the addition of Caste discrimination as a facet of the Protected Characteristic of Race. This came about because a significant proportion of the UK's ethnic minorities are from Hindu backgrounds. It is to be noted that the same protection is not extended to people on account of class/socio-economic background; some would consider that the UK's class system is an informal caste structure. This is expected to be incorporated into statute during the 2015 to 2020 term of the Conservative Government.

Something to consider

A pregnant woman arrived at a hospital about to give birth. She started shouting and screaming at the black Gynaecologist to get out because she only wanted her baby delivered by a white person. The Manager in charge agreed to the request which led then to a complaint of discrimination by the black member of staff.

Was it appropriate to agree to the patients demands?

Our response

Public bodies have an obligation to eliminate discrimination, advance equality of opportunity and promote good relations between people of all Protected Characteristics. As such it could be reasonably argued that, to have a quiet life, the hospital management failed in its duty to show due regard in terms of its obligations to the Black member of staff, under the Equality Act 2010.

Religion and Belief

The Equality Act protects people from discrimination because of religion or religious or philosophical belief. People are also protected from being discriminated against because of lack of religion or belief, so they cannot be treated less favourably because they do not follow a certain religion or have no religion or belief at all.

It is unlawful to treat anybody less favourably because they hold or you think they hold a particular religious or philosophical belief. This does not extend to the practise. For example, a person who is a Seventh Day Adventist applies for a job. The practise of that Faith may be to abstain from working on a Saturday, but Saturday happens to be your busiest day of the week, and you happen to be a very small company who cannot find a reasonable alternative. In this case you do not have to offer the job to the applicant as Saturday working is an essential aspect of the job.

An organised Religion is recognised by having a founder and a set of customs and practises that are engaged in by the followers of the respective religion. This includes all major religions e.g. Judaism, as well as the less widely practised faiths e.g. paganism.

Belief, on the other hand, relates not so much to religion in this context as to a philosophical belief system such as Atheism. To be protected under the UK Equality Act ACAS (the Advisory, Conciliation and Arbitration Service) tells us that a philosophical belief must:

- be genuinely held
- be a belief and not an opinion or viewpoint, based on the present state of information available
- be a belief as to a weighty and substantial aspect of human life and behaviour
- attain a certain level of cogency, seriousness, cohesion and importance
- be worthy of respect in a democratic society, compatible with human dignity and not conflict with the fundamental rights of others

The UK is a multicultural, multi-religious environment and has seen the growth of a number of different types of places of worship since the 1960's. Many workplaces, however, do not offer prayer facilities for employees who are practitioners of a faith or religion. Some employers have extended their prayer facilities to those of no faith or religion who may wish to have space for reflection and thinking. Such extension has proven to be particularly helpful to workers who may have undergone some bereavement or other trauma such as divorce. These rooms are commonly referred to as quiet rooms.

Something to consider

An employee recently converted to orthodox Judaism and approached his manager explaining that he can no longer work from Sunset on a Friday until Sunset on a Saturday. Saturday is one of the business's busiest days. At the same time, another team member requests leave of absence on a Saturday in a few weeks' time because his football team is playing in the Football Association's Semi Final at Wembley Stadium.

Which request would you agree to?

Our response

In this case it would be inappropriate to disregard a person's request to amend working hours that contravene their religion's laid down practices. Therefore, it would be appropriate to decline the team member's request and give priority to the employee who has converted to Judaism.

However, on a longer term basis, a creative solution can be sought that allows other members of the team to have proportionately more Sunday leave which would be accommodated by the Jewish employee who cannot work on Friday Afternoons and Saturdays.

Sex

Sex is the biological classification that distinguishes a man (male) from a woman (female). The law protects both men and women from being treated less favourably on account of their sex. Historically, women have been treated less favourably than men in the workplace. Even at the time of writing, women earn on average at least 12% (some studies claim it is nearer to 22%) less than their male counterparts in like-for-like jobs. Furthermore, and contrary to popular belief, the law also protects men who are treated less favourably when in a minority compared to women in given workplaces.

A more subtle area of discrimination is in the case of part-time workers (the majority of whom are women) who cannot access the same job development and opportunities as their full time counterparts. An employer, for example, may claim that training opportunities are available to all of its staff, but may make them only available at a time that happens to be outside part-time working hours.

Something to consider

A person working for an employment agency was put on a final written warning and threatened with dismissal because he refused to wear a tie to work. The employer felt that it was unprofessional for him not be dressed in business attire but was quite happy for his female colleagues to wear casual t-shirts underneath their jackets.

Is this fair and appropriate?

Our response

This was tested in a tribunal case, Department for Work and Pensions v Matthew Thompson, EAT, it was deemed inappropriate to expect men and women to have different standards of dress code within the workplace.

Sexual Orientation

Sexual Orientation refers to a person's attraction to the men and/or women with whom they may wish to enter into personal, emotional and/or sexual relationships.

Many people have asserted that sexual orientation is not a matter of choice, but rather a natural inclination, and that all sexual orientations are both healthy and respectable.

It is unlawful to treat someone less favourably because they are (or you think they are) gay, bisexual or straight, whether in employment or in the provision of good and services.

Something to consider

A nightclub bouncer working at a gay nightclub complained to her manager that other staff were constantly taunting and teasing her because she was straight. The manager reminded her that in the current economic climate she was lucky to have a job and "anyway they were only having a bit of a joke and meant nothing by it."

What options were available to the worker?

Our response

The characteristic of Sexual Orientation protects 'straight' people as much as it will protect Gay men and Lesbian women. In this case it was inappropriate for the manager to dismiss the legitimate complaint and concern raised by the employee.

Definitions of Discrimination

The Equality Act 2010 covers the following types of unlawful discrimination:

Direct Discrimination

This is where a person treats another person less favourably because of a protected characteristic. This less favourable treatment can be intentional or unintentional.

Something to consider

You advertise for a young Indian female to be a radio presenter to front a breakfast show on your newly launched radio station, *Indibrit FM*. Your reason for wanting an Indian person is based on the need for authenticity.

Would this be acceptable and why?

Our response

The selection criteria appear to show that authenticity from an Indian perspective is required.

Reasons of authenticity may apply, for example, in character roles in cinema or theatre but would not necessarily apply where the role in question is not visible, or apparent, to the audience (service user), especially where a person who may not have the requisite heritage but has the relevant experience and expertise. In the cited example the job advert would be more appropriate if it sought a person who had significant experience of Indian culture and was able to converse in at least two Indian languages.

> It would also be inappropriate to stipulate a gender for this role. However, if the company was significantly under represented by women, the advert could state that, "Applications from Women are welcome as we are currently seeking to create a better gender balance in our organisation."

Indirect Discrimination

This is where a provision or condition is applied and, whilst applicable to everyone, has a less favourable impact on a person or persons sharing one or more protected characteristics.

Whilst direct discrimination is relatively easy to identify and understand, it is the area of indirect discrimination that tends to be an area of confusion for people. Indirect discrimination can, and often does, occur inadvertently.

> **Something to consider**
>
> Your policy states that, in the event of an evacuation, everyone must walk down the fire escape so as to avoid being trapped in the lifts.
>
> **Why might this be considered an example of indirect discrimination?**
>
> **Our response**
>
> This may be direct discrimination against people with a disability, but also indirect discrimination against older people who may have difficulty walking, but are not covered by the definition of Disability as provided in the Equality Act 2010.
>
> Appropriate reasonable adjustments would need to be put in place, such as chair lifts and/or evacuation holding areas.

Discrimination by Association

This is where someone is treated less favourably because they are, or you think they are, associated with a person or persons who have a Protected Characteristic.

> **Something to consider**
>
> You denied permission to an employee who had requested that his working hours be adjusted to allow him to attend to his elderly and disabled parent.
>
> **Was this a reasonable thing to do?**
>
> **Our response**
>
> It depends on the circumstance and critical business needs, for example, if you are operating a time-critical business in which this employee's responsibilities cannot be taken on by anybody else, then it would be appropriate to consider offering him/her alternative work (wherever possible) which would allow him/her more flexibility. If such an option is not available, then the request cannot meet the business need and would then be dealt with under the appropriate HR policy.

Harassment

Harassment can be defined as behaviour of one or more persons, toward another person or persons, that is unwanted, unwelcomed and unreciprocated by the recipient(s). Additionally, it has the effect of making the recipient(s) uncomfortable, aggrieved or otherwise humiliated. Such behaviour may be related to a protected characteristic and could be unintentional; it is the impact on the recipient of such behaviour that is the primary concern.

Harassment can be verbal, physical or sexual, or a combination of these.

Something to consider

You notice at your team meetings that a female employee always chooses to sit the furthest away from a particular male colleague and always tries to avoid meetings at which she knows he will be present.

You ask her if there is a problem and she tells you that he is always looking at her in a funny way but she does not want to cause any trouble. You tell her that it is ok and that she can talk to you about anything.

She confides in you about a time when she was standing at the photocopying machine and he came and brushed his genitals against her as he walked by even though there was plenty of room to get by without touching her.

Would this constitute harassment, and what would you do about it?

Our response

The circumstances would strongly suggest this is a case of sexual harassment and physical harassment because of the way he looked at her and brushed against her. You would need to set about a full investigation. (See chapter 7, diagram 18)

Victimisation

This is where somebody is treated less favourably because they have (or you think they have) complained or raised a grievance against you or others in your organisation. Protection also extends to a person or persons who are treated less favourably because of their support for someone else who has similarly complained or raised a grievance.

Something to consider

You are on a recruitment panel for a promotion and there are three shortlisted candidates. When you review their applications, you suspect that one of them was recently a witness for a complainant in a case of bullying and harassment. Towards the end of the interview, you ask this applicant whether they knew the complainant, and the applicant hesitantly says "yes." This applicant is subsequently not selected for the promotion, and a short while later, you are contacted by HR and informed that you have been named as a respondent to a claim of victimisation.

> **Where do you think you stand in the eyes of the law?**
>
> **Our response**
>
> Even if the intent was not to victimise and the decision to select a more suitable candidate was objectively justified, the final decision was then prejudiced by the fact that you asked a question pertaining to whether or not the candidate knew a previous complainant. From this, the candidate could reasonably assume that they were being victimised for this.
>
> We recommend that, in an interview, you restrict questions to anything that is pertinent and relevant to the job role and person specification.

Other Definitions

Respect

Respect is a regard for the feelings, rights and traditions of others. It is where a person is treated in a manner that they ought to be treated. This means not so much *do unto others as you would have them do unto you*, but rather *do unto others as they would do unto themselves*. In other words treat people the way *they* want to be treated rather than the way *you* want to be treated, or the way you think they want to be treated.

> **Something to consider**
>
> You walk into the lavatory and are a bit taken aback when you see someone washing their feet in the sink. You make an apology and walk out. As you go back to your desk, you mention to your colleague that it is disgusting that Rahim has taken off his shoes and socks and is washing his feet in the sink. Your colleague agrees with you, and as Rahim walks back, shouts out a comment to him about a cheesy smell.
>
> **How does this impact on the respect being given to Rahim, especially as there are no private shower facilities at work?**
>
> **Our response**
>
> Each individual has the right to practice their faith in accordance with the orthodoxy of their religion. If an employer is not able to provide private facilities, then it would be acceptable for Rahim to wash his feet ahead of prayer time in the general facilities made available.
>
> The approach of the colleagues may also lead to a claim of harassment on account of religious discrimination.

Positive Action

Where an organisation is under-represented by people with a Protected Characteristic within the preceding 12 months, the organisation may lawfully provide positive encouragement and training to assist persons from such under-represented groups to competing effectively for vacancies/promotions in that organisation.

> **Something to consider**
>
> You have no women on your board of Directors and have decided to shortlist only women for final interview in order to correct this imbalance.
>
> **What is your legal position?**
>
> **Our response**
>
> You are exposed to claims of sex discrimination by all male candidates whom you systematically failed to shortlist. This is because, whilst positive action would have allowed you to provide encouragement and training to support the under-represented group, it does not give you licence to place a person simply because of their Protected Characteristic.[47]
>
> Having taken the positive action it is recommend that you select, then, *only* on the basis of merit. There are certain exceptions, for example women only parliamentary shortlists.

Positive Discrimination

This is where a person is selected for a job simply because they have a Protected Characteristic, especially when a better-qualified person is available to take the post. This is different to Occupational Requirement which permits the employment of a person who has a particular characteristic for reasons of Authenticity or for matters of personal care. Positive Discrimination is unlawful in the UK, except in specific circumstances.

Occupational Requirement

As there is no definitive list of what an Occupational Requirement is, if a dispute arose, it would need to be tested by a tribunal. Where, however, an employer can demonstrate that it is essential for someone to have a particular Protected Characteristic for a given role, this would be considered to be an Occupational Requirement.

To satisfy the Occupational Requirement condition, an employer must be able to demonstrate that:

* it is a necessary requirement for the job
* articulate the good business reason or legitimate aim(s) for applying the requirement, and
* invoking the requirement is an appropriate and proportionate route to achieve the employer's aim.

It may be, for example, an Occupational Requirement for a person to have a disability to perform a certain role, e.g. being part of a consultative group to assess disability access risks, or for reasons of authenticity, i.e. playing the role of an amputee in a stage play.

Public Sector

For our purposes, we are defining the Public sector as governmental and non-governmental bodies that exist to support public services. This also includes those organisations in the Private sector and the Voluntary sector who are suppliers to the Public sector, e.g. contracted-out refuse-collection services by the local government or catering services at your local hospital.

Dignity

There are many definitions of dignity, but for our purposes we choose to consider dignity as a demonstration of attitudes and behaviour that provides acknowledgement to a person's right not to be judged for their beliefs and values.

Where a person's beliefs and values are likely to contribute to adverse working relationships, these could be seen as antagonistic and contrary to the principle of dignity given above.

Something to consider

Carlos visits the local job centre and when he approaches the desk, the advisor has difficulty understanding his request and so raises her voice and starts speaking very slowly. Carlos is confused by this, thanks her and leaves. He later asks a friend why the local people tend to shout at him so much when all he wants to do is get a job to support his family.

How would you feel if you had been treated in this way?

Our response

How often is it that we find ourselves behaving in a way that may appear to be offensive or patronising to others, when our intent is only to help them?

For example, have you ever noticed that when encountering a blind person with a guide dog, some people will address the dog rather than its owner?

Often intentions can be very honourable but the accompanying behaviour can be quite patronising and undermines the dignity of the person to whom it is directed. When we are unsure about how to respond it is often useful to enquire in a respectful way.

General Duties

The equality act requires that three general duties be executed by all public bodies in the UK, and any private organisations that have contractual service provision relationships with them, commonly known as the Public Sector Equality Duties (PSED). In a nutshell, they are to:

- Eliminate unlawful discrimination, harassment, victimisation and any other conduct prohibited by the Act;
- Advance equality of opportunity between people who share a protected characteristic and people who do not share it; and
- Foster good relations between people who share a protected characteristic and people who do not share it.

Eliminating Unlawful Discrimination

All discrimination is not unlawful. UK legislation requires that all public bodies demonstrate how they are addressing discrimination and or potential discrimination against people with one or more of the nine Protected Characteristics. It is not enough simply to be doing it but public bodies must also show how they are doing it, which is part of the specific duty discussed below. For example, an organisation may have put in place a policy that all car parking spaces be allocated firstly to full time members of the workforce, purely because parking spaces are at a premium and the organisation wanted to ensure that such a valuable perk was fully utilised. This would be unlawful discrimination on account of the protected characteristic of Sex (Gender) because proportionately more women work part-time hours than their male counterparts.

Advancing Equality

Advancing equality of opportunity is then about taking the elimination of unlawful discrimination one step further by seeking to reduce disadvantage; meeting the needs of; and encouraging involvement in public life or in other activities where there are low levels of participation of people with Protected Characteristics. For example, an organisation which has a contractual relationship with a public body has an all Asian ownership. If this organisation has no white people on its board of Directors it must be able to demonstrate that this is not down to unlawful discrimination against white people and that (as part of Advancing Equality) it is taking necessary action to encourage the underrepresented white population to apply for vacancies and/or promotions as they arise. This can be achieved through positive action interventions which provide positive encouragement and/or training to help people compete effectively.

Fostering Good Relations

Fostering good relations is very much to do with raising awareness and improving understanding about the needs of people with differing protected characteristics. For example encouraging a person who has undergone gender reassignment to give a talk to their team about what it meant for them and how it has improved their lives. Another example that we have come across is about a person who was calling on door steps and required to record information about the residents. Often when asking the resident a question about their employment status they were given a response such as "I don't work, I stay at home to mind the children." This operative would then simply say to that person, "I will put down that you are a full time parent." This demonstrated an excellent way of fostering good relations by acknowledging the truth of unpaid work and making the other person (who was often a women likely to be covered by the Protected Characteristic of *Pregnancy and Maternity*) feel much better about themselves.

Specific Duties

Current regulations require public bodies to publish an annual action plan and then to demonstrate due regard by publishing progress made at least once every four years. Good practice recommends that progress is reported annually; we would not, for example, expect to produce financial or management accounts only once every four years.

Due Regard

Having due regard means that public bodies are proactively considering how they implement the General Duties and, in order to do this they need to demonstrate that they are working towards:

- Removing or minimising disadvantages suffered by people due to their protected characteristics;
- Meeting the needs of people with protected characteristics; and
- Encouraging people with protected characteristics to participate in public life or in other activities where such participation is low.

The PSED is very much about ensuring equality not through treating everybody the same but by treating everybody with fairness and equity. Therefore it may involve, for example, providing a transcript of a video that is not subtitled and is being shown as part of a team meeting for a person with a hearing impairment

Reasonable Adjustments

UK equalities legislation has long recognised a principal termed 'Reasonable Adjustment' which applies specifically to people with disabilities. A Reasonable Adjustment is any form of modification relating specifically to enable a disabled person to, for example, execute their job effectively, or to be able to access goods and services. For example a person who has severe arthritis and uses crutches could reasonably expect that their office should be located on the ground floor of a building without lift facilities, whereas that person's predecessor who had no disability may well have had their office on the second floor of the same building. This may appear to be unfair to the person who may be required to surrender their ground floor office and move into the second floor office; it is the organisation's responsibility to ensure that staff are trained in understanding their personal responsibilities for upholding equalities legislation and that they would be personally liable if they were not to comply with such a reasonable request to shift offices.

Institutionalised Discrimination

Institutional discrimination broadens out the original concept of institutional racism, first coined in the 1950's in the USA referring to the differential access, experienced by people of colour, to the goods, services, and opportunities within society. When such differential access becomes integral to institutions, it becomes common practice, making it difficult to rectify. In the UK, this concept first became a factor for UK wide consideration following the death of Stephen Lawrence in 1993 which ultimately led to a public inquiry into the conduct of the police service. The concept can apply to all aspects of difference and hence we would deem it to be institutional discrimination. We explore this further, under 'Institutional Racism', below.

Institutional Racism

"The collective failure of an organisation to provide an appropriate and professional service to people because of their colour, culture or ethnic origin. It can be seen or detected in processes, attitudes and behaviours which amount to discrimination through unwitting prejudice, ignorance, thoughtlessness and racist stereotyping which disadvantage minority ethnic people."

From the Sir William Macpherson report into the murder of teenager, Stephen Lawrence

The key phrases in this quote that warrant attention are:

The collective failure – This means it is not about isolated instances of racism by individuals, but rather issues that perhaps have become the norm in your organisation over many years. For example, requesting minimum grades A to C in GSCE Maths and English even where this is not an actual requirement for the role being advertised.

Processes, attitudes and behaviours – As mentioned earlier in the book, attitudes tend to manifest in behaviour. Processes, which includes any policy, procedure or practice in your organisation, unless reviewed regularly, may well end up being directly or indirectly discriminatory. For example, in times gone by, a job advertisement for a secretary may have expressed under Essential Requirements that "she will have typing speeds of at least 35 words per minute." Note the word "she".

Racist stereotyping – This is where a stereotype, which, although clearly not based in fact, can have an adverse impact on people. For example, in the Stephen Lawrence Inquiry, the unconscious bias demonstrated by the actions of the police officers was that black people were more likely than white people to be trouble makers or criminals.

As alluded to earlier, if we substitute 'racism' from the Macpherson definition for any other 'ism', it quickly becomes apparent that the definition is applicable to any form of unlawful discrimination within an organisation. What's more, institutional discrimination can apply in both employment and customer service.

Something to consider

In one of our training sessions, a female delegate found nothing wrong with members of her team calling her a 'Barbie Doll'.

Do you see anything wrong with this term?

Our response

Discriminatory values and behaviour, when they have gone unchallenged for a long time, eventually acquire acceptance and might be considered 'normal' for an organisation. This does not make it any less discriminatory. So, for example, if the female delegate complained that she had been called a Barbie Doll and you dismiss this as her being too sensitive, you are potentially at risk of a tribunal action. The tribunal could easily rule the term as being a sexist comment which was condoned by the organisation and its officer(s). Individuals who do not challenge such behaviour have often allowed themselves to become desensitised in an effort to fit in and often will not consciously recognise the implicit bias around the stereotype of the blond bimbo.

Whilst the press may sensationalise and ridicule, in their reporting, solitary instances such as the example described above, dismissing it as political correctness gone mad, it is important to note that institutionalised discrimination very often is the cumulative effect of seemingly random instances creating a trend which is then built into the fabric of the organisation.

Human Rights Act

Article 14 of the EC Treaty requires that all rights and freedoms shall be enjoyed 'without discrimination on any grounds such as race, sex, colour, language, religion, political or other opinion, national or social origin, association with a minority, property, birth or other status'.

At the time of writing the UK Government was known to be considering the introduction of a UK Bill of Rights and withdrawing from the sovereignty of the European Court of Human Rights.

Chapter 7

Everything is Fine... Until It's Not

I'm thinking of applying for the new vacant Parent Governor position, he mentioned to the Head Teacher. "Oh, ok then," she responded, with a look on her face that spoke volumes. "Is there a problem?" I asked. "Oh no, Mr Patel, obviously you must do as you wish." Whilst he could not put his finger on it, Mr Patel left feeling like he was not going to be welcomed if he became a Governor at the school...

It is not commonly known that the analogy of an ostrich burying its head in the sand is a fallacy. However, how often is it that, in organisational life, individuals are prone to putting their heads into the sand of make-believe? Suddenly, they then find themselves having to deal with problems that could have been addressed when they were merely challenges, and this often results in excessive costs (both tangible and invisible) to the organisation and the individuals concerned.

In today's world of competing demands, labour shortages and budget cutbacks, it can be very easy to overlook or instigate something that appears to be a quick win, which could be presumed, in hindsight, to be discriminatory. If the 'quick win' backfires you can be faced with costs related to litigation, tribunals and/or criminal action as well as the cost of replacing staff.

By way of example, an employee, John, a gay man, 'came out' to colleagues some months ago. Facing some tacit discrimination, especially by his line manager, John raised a grievance and the outcome was inconclusive. The investigating team did, however, recommend mediation as a preferred solution. The mediation resulted in what may be described as an uneasy truce between the two individuals.

Recently, a vacancy arose for a more senior role in the same department, and John contacted one of this book's authors, who was acting as a mentor, to discuss whether John should apply for the new role. The mentor asked John why he wished to apply for this role while he was actively looking for a post outside his company. John explained that he did not have a specific desire to leave the company, but that his position with his line manager was such that he could not envisage any opportunity for progression. With the new role, whilst he would be still reporting to the existing manager for some aspects of the job, he would be reporting to a new line manager for most of the other aspects of the job. Additionally, in his own eyes, the role was fully within his capability and offered a real prospect for career progression.

On the advice of his mentor, John approached his line manager to let him know that he was going to apply for the more senior role. John described his line manager's reaction as, at best, cool, and perhaps even defensive. John's line manager told John not to expect any favours and that there would be no guarantee he would get the job. John explained that he was not looking for any favours; just a fair chance. In talking to his mentor, John expressed reservations about his line manager's attitude and was advised to go through due process and not to prejudice the situation.

Subsequently, having been interviewed by a panel which included his line manager, John was told that he was unsuccessful in his application. He was given a lot of positive feedback and was advised to take the next-level formal qualification to assist his further progress. Following this, John was informed that the person to whom the role had been offered had decided not to take it up because they wanted to work part time and this was a full-time role. John's line manager further went on to say that this role was now going to external recruitment. Again John was told that he could apply if he wanted to, but with no guarantee, and the fact that he did not have the higher qualification counted against him.

John asked why, if this higher-level qualification was an essential or desirable requirement, this was not stipulated in the role or person specification, to which the manager offered no satisfactory response.

A number of issues come to light in this situation:

- How objective was the laying down of the role specification and person specification?
- How clearly was this communicated in the vacancy advertisement?
- Having not identified a suitable candidate, what else might the recruiter have done to secure the suitable candidate?
- Was the approach to feedback appropriate?
- Why did the line manager have no satisfactory response?
- Was the composition of the interview panel the right composition, given the history between the line manager and John regarding his previous grievance about discrimination?
- What part did unconscious bias play in the decision?

The responses to these questions provides a view as to whether equality, diversity and inclusion principals were integrated into procedure and practice by this employer. Again, we hasten to add that this was an actual case whose details have been modified to protect the guilty and the innocent.

Who, in this situation, had their head in the proverbial sand and why?

In our opinion, the responsibility lay initially with the recruiting line manager who was also on the recruitment panel, and ultimately it is the whole organisation's responsibility. If the line manager had declared their interest and only revealed their assessment of John after the other members of the panel had come to their preliminary conclusion, it would have demonstrated a level of objectivity in the process. Secondly, we would need to understand the level to which the various members of the recruitment panel had been trained in objective assessment; this is where the organisation's responsibility lies. The employer as a whole is accountable for the actions of each of its employees. Employers may discharge such responsibility by taking sufficient steps to ensure its employees are trained in their responsibilities under employment/equality legislation. Some would argue that this is what the HR function is there for. However, increasingly, most of us work in organisations supported by HR business partners whose role it is to *support* managers and staff and *not to carry them*.[48] Even where HR does not operate a business-partner model, it does not remove the accountability of supervisors and managers. Ultimately, discrimination is a criminal act, not a civil act. If you are a line manager applying for a new job and have been involved as a named party in a tribunal claim that was upheld against you, then you are under an obligation to disclose this to a new prospective employer.

This brings us on to considering how best to deal with situations when they are no longer fine. Recognising always that prevention is better than cure, we still need to be cognisant of the need to ensure appropriate measures are in place for when prevention has not been possible, and equality/inclusion has potentially been breached.

I Call a Spade a Spade

Most of us want clarity and openness in our working relationships. As a manager or supervisor, our focus is often simply on getting things done. Issues arise when it is forgotten that managers are not only responsible for getting things done, but also for the people that make things happen. This can create a pressurised situation where our stress-induced behaviour comes to the forefront, our innate/unconscious biases manifest and potentially lead to grievances or complaints of discrimination. In a majority of cases, discrimination was not the intent of the manager concerned. Of course, there is always a minority that will, for a variety of reasons, seek to harass, bully or victimise others either in the workplace or in the provision of customer service.

Regardless of the underlying reasons, in our experience it always seems to come as a shock when a manager is called in by someone in Human Resources to inform them that a grievance has been raised against them; it is especially so when the grievance is deemed serious enough to warrant the suspension of the respondent who is, more often than not, a person in a more senior role than the complainant. It can often lead to a sense of indignant outrage *that anybody dares even challenge the way I am doing my job. After all, nobody knows the pressure that I am working under. HR have no idea of the type of morons that I have to deal with and now they want to take their word over mine.*

I Just Want It To Stop

On the other side, a grievance or complaint is likely, in the majority of cases, to be a last desperate call for help by someone who simply wants the perceived inappropriate behaviour to stop. It usually takes an extreme amount of effort on the part of a complainant to actually muster the courage to raise the grievance in the first place. This is because of fears surrounding whether or not it will affect their ongoing career prospects, whether they will be believed and whether they should simply resign and find another job because the stress of the situation has become too much.

Of course, there is always a small proportion of complainants who may be acting vexatiously (acting either consciously or unconsciously for the purpose of creating frustration and/or to vex the respondent or the organisation) and there will be others who are acting in earnest, but are seen to be acting vexatiously.

Oh No, Not Again!

How often is it that, in the midst of countless workforce issues HR personnel are required to manage, suddenly they are presented with a complaint or grievance that has reached a point of no return?

"Don't these managers ever listen to what we have to say?"

and

"Why is it that we have to fix the world's problems? They seem to think that we have nothing better to do than to sort out the mess that they get themselves in to."

Or,

"Here we go again… another complaint from X. I wonder if they don't have anything better to do than to raise complaints against other members of staff, especially when I have so much on my plate at the moment. This is going to take a huge amount of management time, and why can't they learn to deal with these things before they become a really big problem?"

Power Play

In all of the above situations, you can perhaps get an appreciation of the underlying positions of the complainant, the respondent and the HR professional. Many a time, issues of discrimination are the product of someone in a position of power behaving inappropriately to someone who does not wield the same level of power. The power is not necessarily related to seniority within the organisation. Power is, however, a major lever that can be used or abused to promote diversity and discrimination respectively. Power may be defined in the following ways:

Position Power – this is where a person is in a more senior role and responsible for the actions of another. Such power can create a sense of obligation in people where they feel no choice but to comply with the person holding the position power.

Connection Power – this is where an individual (either consciously or unconsciously) takes advantage of people or situations because of their actual or perceived connections with those in more influential roles or positions.

Expert Power – this is where a person has acquired a level of expertise that can make them relatively indispensable and uses this as a lever for fair or unfair advantage over others.

Knowledge Power – this is where (unlike expert power) an individual is in possession of information or knowledge that could be used, for example to intimidate/manipulate others. This could involve personal knowledge of another's situation or indeed of the organisation.

Legitimate Power – this is where, owing to their position, a person has both organisational and actual authority over people and situations.

Referent Power – this is where a person does not necessarily have legitimate power, but carries influence owing to the fact that they are well respected by most of the people with whom they interact in the workplace.

Reward Power – this is where a person has the ability to bestow rewards, and is often related to legitimate power, but can also be linked to connection power.

Power play is highly likely a cause for discriminatory behaviour by those in a position of control and influence (those perpetrating power play) against people who do not possess similar power.

By way of an example, we could consider a live situation involving a very senior executive and his female PA. The executive knew that his PA was gay but had not 'come out' to colleagues at work.

The executive not only had position power but knowledge power, too, over his PA, which he then brought to bear, leading to the executive subtly coercing the PA to work unreasonably long hours and at weekends. The PA had a grave concern but little influence or control over the situation. The executive took full advantage of the control he held and used it to influence, intimidate and ultimately violate the PA's dignity. As mentioned, the PA had very little control or influence other than to raise a complaint or resign. Our experience shows that in such situations, the employee is more likely to resign than go through the stress of a grievance procedure.

In terms of control, the individual holding the power is more likely to hold formal direct line responsibility (e.g. line manager) or indirectly, e.g. where a person reports to another for just a part of their role (e.g. a project manager). Others not in such a direct or indirect position wield influence more informally in power plays. Such positions of control and influence will clearly have a bearing on the integration of equality, diversity and inclusion.

From this, it can be seen how important the role of leaders and managers becomes in engendering an environment where equality, diversity and inclusion can thrive. It is often assumed that such individuals will know how to implement and sustain equality, diversity and inclusion. Most of us are often told that it is simply a matter of common sense, but, of course, *everything is fine until it is not.*

When things are not OK, a commonly used default position is to refer to the organisation's HR department. In an ideal world, HR departments and managers would be holding a position of interdependence to be able to support line management and staff equally. In our experience, it is not unusual to find that the HR default position is more to defend the organisation and the management (even where management clearly are behaving inappropriately) rather than to independently support both management and staff. However, if organisations (and this does not mean HR exclusively) were to provide the appropriate training, support and cultural environments in which all individuals could challenge appropriately, this would reduce the need for HR to take such a defensive stance.

What is Appropriate Challenge?

Where appropriate challenge is encouraged, it will be relatively easy for individuals to speak out, without fear of recrimination, when another's words or behaviours are causing offence. In many teams and organisations, people live constantly in fear of whether they may be upsetting someone else. This leads to a culture in which people consider political correctness to have gone mad. In actuality, if a person was to say something or behave in a particular way within a culture where appropriate challenge was the accepted norm, then issues would be nipped in the bud before they became problems. For example, one colleague refers to another as fat. In the medical model, being fat or obese is seen generally through the lens of body mass index. However, the same term is a relative concept when we consider a societal model. If somebody told you that the term fat was inappropriate term to use, you may become defensive. However, if you were to simply consider how this might make the other person feel, you would start choosing your words more carefully.

The difference between challenge being aggressive or appropriate can often be a very fine distinction. A challenge may be seen as a personal attack by the person being challenged and they may then respond with a personal attack on the challenger...."Can't you take a joke......," "I meant nothing by it.....," etc. Many times the person being offensive is blissfully ignorant of the offence they are causing and this is why they will tend to react negatively to the challenger.

However, when challengers can challenge by describing the impact on themselves, it is often easier for the person creating the 'offence' to understand the inappropriateness of their words/ behaviours. For example, if a person is laughing about a racist comment made by a comedian on the TV the previous evening, and a colleague expresses that such a jokes makes them feel degraded and or undermined, the statement is appealing to the other's sense of dignity and respect rather than creating blame. Of course, if the other, in this case, continues with that behaviour, they are now on notice that they are potentially culpable for harassment.

It is an accepted fact that ignorance of the Law is no defence, therefore, especially when we have been made aware, the duty of care to not be discriminatory falls on us. Ignore another's appropriate challenge at your own risk. Most organisations will have a Dignity and Respect policy together with examples of appropriate and inappropriate words and behaviours. Often individuals and groups that are in the majority may make accusations of political correctness gone mad. This can be because the individuals concerned do not necessarily appreciate the way in which certain words and behaviours are 'loaded'. For example men are 'studs' but women are 'sluts'. This is covered in more detail in Chapter 1. *The basis of perception.* Why is it that a promiscuous man can boast of his achievements but a similar women should be made to feel ashamed of them?

When all employees in an organisation are encouraged to make appropriate challenge and not to make the challenger 'wrong' this will, over a period of time, become a new cultural norm for the organisation and will avoid or reduce the number of grievances and complaints that may have to be dealt with.

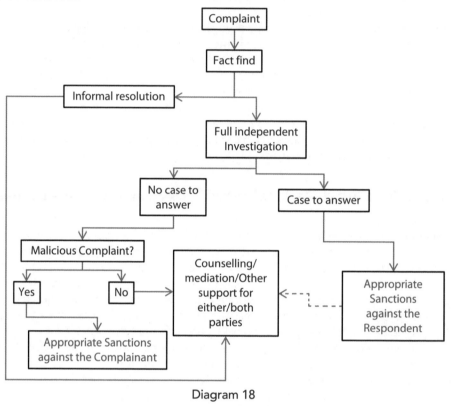

Diagram 18

The Route through a Complaint / Grievance

Given that the ideal and the principle of appropriate challenge is still a far-off destination and that we must deal with reality as it currently stands, it becomes more important to understand how issues may be dealt with, both formally and informally, to allow both staff and management to feel safe and protected. Diagram 18 details, as a starting point, a generic view of the route that many organisations can follow when dealing with a complaint of discrimination based on any of the 9 Protected Characteristics:

Complaint

The complaint or grievance may be either formal or informal and could be received by anybody in the organisation. The inherent danger here is that it is ignored because the complainant says that they don't wish to do anything about it. However the greater responsibility is to ensure the wellbeing of all employees.

Fact Find

Once a complaint or grievance has been identified and lodged it needs to be decided whether to do an informal fact find or to go straight to formal investigation. This will need to be determined by the seriousness of the complaint. HR will be able to advise.

Informal Resolution

If a fact find is conducted and the outcome is that an informal resolution is appropriate (and the complainant concurs), then you can go straight to resolution, which may involve mediation and/or other remedies.

The ACAS code of practice, issued in 2009[49] on disciplinary and grievance procedures requires that employers and employees should do all that they can to resolve disciplinary and grievance issues themselves and should consider using a third party (for example a mediator or an arbitrator) to help resolve the problem, ending up in an employment tribunal as a very last resort. Such measures may include counselling, mediation, re-training and/or other appropriate interventions to help resolve the situation.

Informal resolution could follow a fact-find or post a full independent investigation.

Full Independent Investigation

Where a fact find reveals the need for a more formal full investigation, this should, ideally, be executed by an independent person who is competent in conducting investigations. In an ideal world, objectivity can be demonstrated through appointing an investigator who is not an employee of the same organisation. This may not always be feasible, in which case a senior person from a non-related department or function who is trained in investigation skills ought to be employed to conduct such investigation.

For smaller organisations, there is the added risk of not having sufficient people available to undertake investigations, and it may be that they can set up bilateral or multilateral arrangements with other companies of a similar size. Of course, whoever is used needs to have been trained.

No Case to Answer

Having conducted either a fact find or a full investigation, the complaint may not be upheld. In such cases, it must then be determined whether or not the complaint was malicious. The complainant will also have the right to appeal the finding in line with their organisation's policy and procedures.

Additionally, the complainant should also be given information on how to appeal such finding should they wish to. The complainant should not have to research appeal procedures independently....they often are in a state of high stress at this point.

Case to Answer

If the investigation upholds the complaint, then appropriate sanctions against the respondent will need to be considered, decided upon and implemented.

Malicious Complaint

On some occasions it may be determined that the complainant behaved maliciously towards the respondent. In such instances, whatever sanction may have been applicable to the respondent, had the complaint been upheld, would now be applicable to the complainant.

Appropriate Sanctions Against the Respondent

Following an investigation, which concludes that there is a reasonable belief that the discriminatory behaviours took place, sanctions must be appropriate to the severity of the situation. Sanctions may range from a verbal warning all the way to summary dismissal. More detail about this can be found in any good employee relations text book.

The complainant will not be informed of the sanctions applied to the respondent owing to employer-employee confidentiality issues. This can feel quite unfair to the complainant, however, a good employee handbook will often provide the types of sanction that could/would be applied in certain situations. For example, a publicly available document from Portsmouth University[50] states:

> *"Sanctions*
>
> *Bullying and harassment potentially constitute gross misconduct and, therefore, if a complaint is upheld it could lead to the dismissal of a member of staff or the exclusion of a student. Where dismissal or exclusion are not considered appropriate, the implications for continued work and study relationships will be given serious consideration by the Director of Human Resources (staff) or the Academic Registrar (students) and appropriate action taken.*
>
> *The University will not move the person who has complained of bullying or harassment in this case, unless it is at their request. If it is felt advisable to separate the two parties, consideration will be given to appropriate action that provides a safe inclusive working and learning environment for all concerned."*

Appropriate Sanctions Against the Complainant

Earlier, we alluded to malicious complaints. Where there is no case to answer, but it is deemed that the complaint was malicious, then the same sanction would apply against the complainant as would have been applicable to the respondent if the complaint had been upheld.

This concludes the explanations of the aspects provided in the diagram.

Prevention versus Cure

Whilst organisations often find themselves needing a cure, clearly proactivity is far more beneficial than reactivity. The view of many tribunals has been that the majority of cases could have been resolved had they been dealt with at the earliest stages. Of course, this relies on the organisation fostering a culture where issues may be raised without fear of recrimination. This can only occur where there is common understanding, mutual dignity and respect, and clear effective communication.

What, then, are appropriate preventative measures that will engender such an environment?

When we consider prevention, it is worthwhile noting that no preventative measures are ever 100% fool-proof. However, the measures applied will serve very well in minimising the impact of discrimination and unconscious bias in the workplace and in the provision of goods and services. Some such preventative measures will include the following:

Policy and Procedures

Well-considered and appropriately-drafted policies and procedures will have integrated principles that make equality and diversity issues clear and leave little scope for ambiguity. In this way, individuals know where they stand and what standards are expected of them.

Of course, even the best written policies and procedures have no value if they are not easily accessible. Many large organisations now make policies and procedures available on their intranets. Another option is to provide employees with PDF versions that can be emailed where a central portal is not available.

Inclusion and Ostracism

Inclusion and ostracism can be considered as polar opposites; the first brings individuals together and the second creates division. There should not be an undue reliance on policy and procedure to create a culture of inclusivity; it is incumbent on leaders to be effective role models who are prepared to consider each individual in line with their strengths and capabilities, rather than their personal likes and dislikes. Furthermore, ostracism would be regarded as a form of bullying and/or victimisation.

The "I"[51] in Teams

Most of us have heard the cliché that there is no 'I' in 'team'. With due respect, we seek to challenge this. An effective team makes full use of the strengths and qualities of each 'I' in that team. This starts to create a one-organisation culture, rather than a one-culture organisation.[52] If we were to take the example of a soccer team, and we decided that there is no 'I' in the team, then we would not be developing the best goalkeeper, the best defender, the best midfielder or the best striker. This is a key principle of valuing diversity.

An effective team is really not a homogeneous mass that has lost the identity of the individuals within it. To be effective each 'I' in the team needs to be aware of any cultural sensitivities important to other "I's" that need to be respected. Thus, it is not appropriate to think that in an effective team, everyone must go to the pub on a Friday evening, for example. Where an environment of mutual dignity is prevalent, we are able to engender team spirit by respecting individual traditions, beliefs and circumstances. A single dad, for example, may only see his children from Friday to Sunday and, wishing to maximise his available time with them, may choose to forego a Friday night at the pub.

Leading from the Front

Throughout this book we have been at pains to emphasise the role of leadership in establishing and maintaining an appropriate culture that allows equality of opportunity and equality of service. Diversity and Inclusion are principles that cannot be encapsulated by legislation alone. In Chapter 6, we saw that the law attaches to Level 3 of Gordon Allport's model, namely Discrimination. The law provides penalties in the wake of evidence pointing to adverse treatment because of a protected characteristic. Leading from the front means being prepared to challenge the status quo when it does not promote the rights of all stakeholders in an organisation. Furthermore, Diversity and Inclusion are clearly about everybody, although particular attention will need to be given to those who have been subject to the adverse effects of discrimination that has been ongoing for tens if not hundreds of years. As mentioned earlier, current legislation permits organisations to provide encouragement and/or training for protected groups that have been underrepresented during the previous 12 months. Strong leaders will therefore not shy away from implementing well thought out and appropriate positive action measures that provide training and encouragement to under-represented groups to compete effectively for promotions and other vacancies as they arise.

Employee Assistance Provision

Employee assistance provision may be seen as an effective route to prevention. The major advantage of using external EAPs is that they are independent and preserve the privacy of the individual under normal circumstances. All EAPs commit to feeding back broad themes, that they are dealing with, to the commissioning organisation. This empowers organisations' Leadership to make informed decisions around managing Diversity and Inclusion, whilst still maintaining individual confidentiality. This gives staff far more confidence in raising concerns before they turn into major problems. Whilst EAPs carry a cost, often this cost is far more preferable to the visible and invisible costs of defending a tribunal action.

Partnership Working (Managers and HR)

Many organisations now work in a structure where HR business partners support line management. However, in practice it seems that it is still the HR manager that will be taking a lead as opposed to supporting the line manager. This is particularly so in the event of complaints and investigations. If manager and HR Partner were to work together more proactively, to promote and support the one-organisation culture this would, over time, result in a reduction in the number of discrimination, bullying and victimisation issues that have to be dealt with formally. Unfortunately, most organisations' HR professionals are still regarded as second-class citizens and a cost to the business. This totally circumvents most assertions that 'people are our greatest asset', purely because line management does not know, or has never been taught, how to work in partnership with its HR business partner to develop its people.

So this brings us full circle to the title of this chapter. Indeed, everything is fine until, unfortunately, it does go wrong. In a *one-organisation* culture (as opposed to a *one-culture* organisation) where dignity and respect are the order of the day, supported through objective selection, recruitment and promotion, as well as strong leadership and effective teamwork, the incidences of things going wrong will be minimised. It is easier to start from a clean sheet of paper, but of course most organisations already have lots of scribbles on their piece of paper, which only start to be erased when tribunals demand it. As we have pointed to earlier, it is better to implement a culture of prevention rather than a culture of correction. This really does require effective leadership and pragmatic partnership with HR. Ultimately, this will engender a one-organisation culture.

But... perhaps the overriding message of this chapter is that there is absolutely no room for complacency to set in.

Chapter 8

Practice makes...

It's all very well you telling me that I should be doing things differently, but what should I do and why should I bother. I mean, does it really make a difference?

It can be very confusing thinking about what needs to change and how to bring it about. Here below we give some examples of things done by real people in real organisations. Hopefully this will give you some inspiration to think about what you could achieve. As for the question about whether it makes a difference, we would direct you to the anecdote at the end of this chapter.

The Open University – *Aspire~* Leadership and Mentoring Programme for minority staff

The Open University (OU) is the biggest university in the UK and Europe, with over 170,000 students. It is one of, if not the, premier distance learning organisation in the world. The university found that:

Our annual OU monitoring information and research showed that ethnic minority internal staff at the OU reported barriers to career progression and had a higher intention to leave the University

Further qualitative research was carried out which identified that ethnic minority employees felt that promotion procedures were operating fairly, but that they lacked access to influential networks of decision makers. As a result, they had less confidence in putting themselves forward for career development opportunities and were less likely to be recognised as capable if they did.

The Resolution
A targeted intervention that addresses the needs and concerns of affected staff. In the light of the data analysis, and further qualitative research, the OU commissioned one of the authors to work with the Equality and Diversity Team, Human Resources, senior staff and the co-Chairs of the BME staff network, to design a programme that specifically addressed these areas for concern.

How the resolution was implemented
Eleven mentees were selected through a competitive application process, and then matched with 11 senior mentors from across the OU for its pilot programme between February and November 2011. Aspire~ offered participants:

- Start-up induction workshop
- Mid-programme workshop

- One-to-one monthly mentoring meetings
- A dedicated Programme Coordinator to run the workshops, act as a central point of contact and to help resolve any issues and keep partnerships on track

Aspire~ had the full backing of OU senior leaders, with the Vice-Chancellor launching it in December 2010 and presenting completion certificates at the Celebration Event on 18 January 2012.

Typically, a programme of this size would expect for one or two partnerships to not run the full course. All of the Aspire~ mentoring partnerships stayed together for the duration of the nine month pilot, which is testament to the dedication of all involved, and the value mentees and mentors were experiencing.

The positive impact for the organisation:

Aspire~ received overwhelming positive feedback from the mentees:

- Strong support of their personal and professional development and career direction
- Increased confidence in themselves and their value to the OU
- Opportunities to learn from peer insight and experiences
- Greater awareness of development opportunities

Mentors were also overwhelmingly positive about *Aspire~*:

- Found mentor partnerships constructive, useful and positive
- Aspire~ demonstrated the OU's serious commitment to creating an inclusive environment and addressing the experiences of its ethnic minority employees
- 10 out of 11 mentors were willing to serve as mentors again

Analysis of the OU's research pointed to similar experiences for disabled internal staff and, because the pilot programme proved to be so successful, it was extended to disabled internal staff. Tweaks to the programme included wider networking opportunities with mentors, peers and senior leaders. Further, mentees completing the base programme were invited to enter a second nine month programme, *Aspire~Plus*, focusing on second stage leadership development.

Over a four-year period, over 50 people had been through the programme and, since launch, something approaching 1 in 3 participants had successfully achieved career related moves.

At the time of writing this book the programme was under review to consider how it may be able to add further value to Mentees and Mentors.

Southern Health NHS Foundation Trust – Quality Care When And Where You Need It

Southern Health NHS Foundation Trust provides community health, specialist mental health and learning disability services for people across Hampshire, Dorset, Oxfordshire and Buckinghamshire. It is one of the largest providers of these types of service in the UK and employs some 9,000 staff. Southern identified that:

In order to better serve our customers (patients) we wanted to:

- enable staff to connect with the vision, values and related behaviours expected from the organisation

- meet the quality, safety, operational and financial obligations facing the organisation in a fair and equitable way, and
- attract, develop and retain skilled and committed people to the organisation

All of the above needed to be achieved within the context of increasing financial constraint; a changing regulatory framework being introduced by the Care Quality Commission; the introduction of a new mandatory equality framework (the Equality Delivery System – EDS2) and Workforce Race Equality Standard (WRES); and the underpinning requirements of the public sector equality duty arising from the Equality Act 2010.

The Resolution
To drive equality, diversity and inclusion through performance via:

- Governance and reporting
- Organisational and cultural development
- Workforce and customer engagement
- Learning, education and development
- Employee relations

An internal Equality Standard was created in order to embed a sustainable service delivery model for equality, diversity and inclusion. The aim was to mainstream the EDS2 and WRES, clinical and corporate services work towards detailed standard criteria and offer incremental recognition of improvement with three levels of award: bronze, silver and gold.

How the resolution was implemented
The Equality Standard toolkit includes a guidance document outlining standard criteria and a Provider Compliance Assessment (PCA) to record evidence.

Southern Health launched the Equality Standard within their clinical and corporate service areas and performance was managed locally at mainstream business meetings overseen by nominated equality impact leads. Each service was required to submit evidence against the criteria in the standard and progress reports were submitted to a trust-wide equality impact group (EIG) before going to the Trust Board.

The Equality Standard

- provides a single reference point incorporating all elements of the Equality Act 2010 and EDS2;
- aims to significantly impact upon the way EDS2 is integrated into everyday business activity;
- provide clinical and corporate services with a toolkit to plan and monitor their work on equality and diversity;
- outline the key criteria services will work towards and the level of evidence provided will determine the standard level achieved; and
- identify our performance and raise standards in equality and diversity practice
- Improve organisational response to legal, commissioner and regulatory requirements

The positive impact for the organisation:

1. Each clinical and corporate business area evidencing their equality and diversity performance
2. 50% reduction in the involvement of BME staff in formal disciplinary process

3. 24% increase in total workforce reporting to disability status
4. 20% increase in total workforce reporting to sexual orientation status
5. 19% increase in total workforce reporting to religion or belief status
6. 300 diversity champions (VOX POP) across the organisation

The Co-operative – Quality support as the workforce ages

The Co-operative has over 3,750 high street branches in the UK. In addition to retail products and groceries, they also supply financial services, travel, funeral care and legal services. They identified that:

The UK has an ageing population and state pension age is rising, meaning that people need to extend their working lives. For this to happen, workforces need to be proactive to support older employees. As the organisation's workforce ages, particularly over the next 10 years, it is important to understand our colleagues more proactively, especially in respect of retention, skills, knowledge and motivational factors. Also, the longer term impact on people in their 30s and 40s, a sandwich generation [i.e. people who have both elder care and younger care to address], and challenges colleagues may face to continue their employment. Having a better understanding of these issues will enable us to look at how we as an organisation can support this.

The Resolution
A three year study started two years ago, in 2014, in partnership with a local University.

This involved having a PhD student working with us over that period. Investigating HR data and interviewing colleagues to understand our own community. This insight has also allowed us to overlap into other areas and understand vulnerability of certain demographics. The overall aim of the research is to explore the factors that enable or inhibit people to work for longer, post traditional retirement age, in a large UK based private sector retail organisation such as the Co-operative

How the resolution was implemented
Phase One – was an extensive quantitative analysis based on three years' HR data, as well as a longitudinal multivariate [ie, based on two or more variables] analysis. In the first instance the project explored a number of business (for example, salary, job type) and demographic variables (for example, gender, region) impacting on levels of sickness absence (a key indicator of health and extended working lives) in people aged 50s.

Phase Two – was informed by the key findings at Phase One of the project and comprises two qualitative studies:

Phase Two: Study 1 - face to face interviews with 15 Greater Manchester based employees over 60 years old

- This study explores the experiences of colleagues who are approaching traditional retirement age in order to inform future practice and support.

Phase Two: Study 2 – face to face interviews with 15 supervisors involved in supporting older workers

- This study explores the experiences of colleagues supporting/supervising those who are approaching traditional retirement age in order to inform future practice and support for employees.

The positive impact for the organisation

- To be more proactive
- To take an independent view of our policies and processes and if necessary change
- To have a clear understanding of expectation from colleagues
- To engage with the wider community

EY – Black and Minority Ethnic (BME) Leadership Programme

EY, previously Ernst and Young, is a global financial and professional services organisation. In 2015, EY opened its first ever global Security Operations Centre at Thiruvananthapuram, Kerala in India and will invest $20 million over 5 years to combat increasing threat of cybercrimes. EY in the UK identified that:

At EY, BME, senior representation was low, attrition high, and role models invisible; our people survey showed BME satisfaction with career progression was low; and our marketplace was globalising. In other words, our BME population was not achieving its potential with us.

As a progressive organisation we needed to invest in BME careers, despite a lack of clarity about how the programme could make a difference and very high levels of discomfort (including in the participants) caused by a preconception that the programme was remedial.

However, our leading work on unconscious bias, our Career Watch programme (to remove career obstacles for underrepresented groups) and our established women's leadership programme indicated to us that our people (and our leaders) were ready to be educated about successful different styles of leadership. We believed that by provoking discussion on BME career development we could focus attention on it – and make change happen.

The resolution

From research we know that if senior roles are not held by diverse leaders, those who are underrepresented can perceive their own difference (be that gender, race, sexual orientation, or a combination of identities) as a threat, even if at the unconscious level. This leads to them downplaying that aspect of who they are, resulting in less disclosure, less trust, weaker relationships, less willingness to take risks, more desire to conform. A recipe for maintaining the status quo.

So we developed a BME Leadership Programme which supports our BME high performers to embrace their difference in a positive way and to use that difference to excel at EY, thus interrupting the status quo.

It is a holistic programme aimed at our highest performing and most senior BMEs. It includes 360 assessment, a two day offsite workshop, individual coaching and exposure to leadership opportunities. The programme builds confidence, and allows people to explore a diverse range of effective leadership styles and understand the inherent difference in strategies adopted by different cultures. It is not a BME cohort for a standard leadership programme although some of the soft skills it addresses could be found in other programmes. It equips people to focus on their future development and creates a collegiate peer network. Careers are transformed by the experiences received during the programme.

Programmes for ethnic minorities exist, but none which include such depth of academic research and such a focus on authentic leadership from a BME point of view. The link to our global market is explicitly made so that our BMEs really understand their role in our future growth plans. We use sophisticated tools to understand the impact of cultural heritage on leadership styles, and to tailor the programme.

Importantly, the programme will lead to sustained change as the participants first realise and then enthusiastically adopt their position as role models to other BMEs in the firm.

An additional benefit is that the organisational learning taking place amongst our leaders, who are starting to understand the real issues surrounding BME career progression and to commit to action.

The positive impact for the organisation

We have achieved great results in the seven years the programme has been running. Not only does workshop feedback indicate extremely high levels of satisfaction, but we have robustly analysed the BMELP participants in comparison with their high performing white and BME peers and can show in the most recent measurement that they are more likely to

- Stay with the firm (96% compared to 91%/88%)
- Retain or improve their (already high) performance rating (36% compared to 11%/5%)
- Be promoted (15% compared to 13%/8%)

Participants are more visible and have been inspired to mentor other BMEs, leading to a formal BME mentoring programme by BMELP participants of their more junior BME colleagues.

In addition, BME and white partners have stepped forward to become role models and support the programme. Our leaders articulate the business case more confidently and actively watch BME careers. Our networks are inspired and our pipeline contains strong BME leaders of the future.

In short, by supporting our BMEs to achieve their potential we are starting to change the culture of our organisation.

E.ON – Improved Diversity Recruitment Drive

E.ON is one of the UK's leading power and gas companies. E.ON operates in over 30 countries and serves over 33 million customers. The E.ON brand continues to service the downstream business including retail and distribution, as well as the Climate and Renewables business; with the upstream business, to be branded *Uniper*, containing all conventional power generation and current Energy Trading activities. They found that:

When our diversity survey highlighted fair recruitment as an opportunity to both increase our penetration into untapped talent pools and build an organisation that is more reflective of society, E.ON responded by redesigning the entire recruitment and selection training programme.

We needed to improve the confidence, calibre and competence of hiring managers in order to increase inclusivity within the talent pool. This required that we embed the principles of fair recruitment and add a focus on reducing unconscious bias in order to improve the application to hire ratio of disabled colleagues.

The resolution

We introduced 'Licence to Recruit', the new E.ON recruitment and selection training programme. It represents significant investment from the UK and is one of only a few mandated training roll-outs between 2013 and 2015.

The training consists of:

- Six e-learning modules
- One day workshop delivered by an external supplier
- Additional support via the Global Recruitment Services team and the E.ON Recruitment portal page.

This training has been available from 2014 and, since April 2015, it has been company policy that at least one manager present at an interview must be 'licenced to recruit'. So far:

- 72% of managers have been trained – other global initiatives have attracted c11%
- Managers from 52 locations and 10 E.ON divisional areas have been trained
- 1,040 managers were trained by the end of 2015

The positive impact for the organisation

The results have been staggering; the application to hire ratio [gap between] disabled [and non disabled] colleagues improved from 70% to 12.5%

This represents a threefold increase in the conversion rate.

Shell - Be Yourself[53]

Royal Dutch Shell plc, commonly known as Shell, is an Anglo–Dutch multinational oil and gas company headquartered in the Netherlands and incorporated in the United Kingdom. Shell employs some 90,000 employees who work in over 70 countries. They recognised that:

One of Shell's core values is that people work together best when all are able to be who they really are but it understands that many people, especially those who are living with a disability, find this hard to do.

The Resolution

Be Yourself[54] is an innovative and interactive approach to help disabled employees be themselves at work featuring a series of short films from 15 Shell employees with a disability, across different geographies, and with different impairments. The shared message is about why it's important to be yourself at work. The campaign was launched to coincide with the United Nations International Day of Persons with Disabilities on 3rd December 2013.

How the Resolution was implemented

Working collaboratively, the four different enABLE networks (employee disability networks) within Shell in the UK, US, Canada and The Netherlands identified employees to be interviewed. *Be Yourself* was positioned as an opportunity for employees to tell their story, explain how they manage their impairment, and why it is important to *be yourself*.

The internal communications department filmed the stories, got them subtitled and edited. IT resources created a website to host the content.

Smaller organisations with limited budgets can do the same for less simply using personal phones and tablets to record the video message and then hosting the content either through an existing website, or through an existing external platform, such as You Tube. The cost need not be restrictive. Once there is agreement for the concept in principle, there is the opportunity to be creative and use technology savvy employees to help bring it to fruition.

The positive impact for the organisation

For Shell the Be Yourself platform has given employees the confidence to share information about their impairment for the first time. This has been achieved through the power of storytelling and drawing inspiration from other Shell employees talking about their experiences.

> "Sharing information let me be who I am. I'm bringing my whole self to work,"
>
> Jannifer Rios.

> "Sharing information for me is a way to prevent barriers being formed. If people know what my limitations are they will work around them as well as I do, which is beneficial for both of us. My autism is part of who I am and has also produced positive things. I'm autistic like I'm Dutch, like I'm an engineer, like I'm tall – it's just part of me."
>
> Diederik Weve, chair of enABLE (disability) network in the Netherlands

> "To enable the company to win, we need to be attractive and inclusive to diverse talent, and that includes people with disabilities. This is all about helping people to perform better, about our leadership attributes of performance and authenticity, and about our core value of respect for people. So I say: 'just be yourself'."
>
> Jorrit van der Togt, Executive Vice President for Human Resources Strategy and Internal Communications.

Microsoft – Apprentice Scheme for BME students

Microsoft is a global leader in IT and aims to be more diverse and inclusive and a role model for the IT sector. Microsoft has an Apprentice Scheme which is suitable for 16 to 24 year olds. Microsoft identified that:

We wanted more students and teachers from BME backgrounds to explore Microsoft as a company, its Apprentice Scheme and the IT sector in general.

The Resolution

In February 2016, Microsoft organised a Student Day for 90+ Black, Asian and other Minority Ethnic students and their teachers from London, Luton and Birmingham.

How the Resolution was implemented?

The day was designed to provide students and teachers with a forum to learn new skills, implement those skills, explore opportunities and have fun. The event involved the following principles: -

- LEARN - Microsoft held 3 specialist talks on App Design, Project Management and Sales and Marketing.
- IMPLEMENT - The students were then required to implement the knowledge in a work environment by creating a Super App (an App that was likely to impact lives, businesses, environment or the way people function). Students were required to work in teams, organise and lead, manage time, be creative and present their ideas to an audience. The winners were awarded trophies, X box console and X box games.
- EXPLORE - There were talks on the Apprentice Scheme, an opportunity to meet employees, apprentices, interns and graduates, a tour of the Campus, product demonstrations (i.e. HoloLens) and use of technologies (i.e. Surface Pro 3 and Office).
- FUN - Students and teachers were engaged in Q&A sessions, a fun quiz and use of Microsoft X Box room. Students and teachers were also given Microsoft branded gifts such as T-shirts, power packs, note pads, pens etc.

The positive impact for the organisation:

75% of attendees completed feedback forms:

- 100% said they would recommend the Student Day to others.
- 96% rated the day as 8, 9 or 10. (10 being outstanding).
- 78% said they would now apply for Microsoft's Apprentice Scheme.

Shorof Uddin, Senior Investigations Manager at Microsoft said, "The student day has proven to be an exceptional success and is a great foundation for us to build an even more diverse workforce at Microsoft."

Chapter 9

The Transience of Diversity

"Well, that's not very diverse of you, is it!", she was heard saying to him. He was left wondering, "what does being diverse mean?" After all we are all diverse beings in a diverse multicultural, multi-ethnic world.

According to dictionary definitions, diversity is about difference and we know that differences are not always constant; I may still feel like I am 25 years old but when somebody calls me uncle who happens to be a 20 something year old the difference becomes apparent. Difference is also transient; it is temporary, constantly changing. Thus, it asks a question: is 'diversity' just the latest buzzword that is widely misunderstood? We hear the term 'diversity' all the time and sometimes it seems to be seen as a general *evil* for all things politically incorrect. However, as we have explored throughout this book, the principles of Diversity, Equality and Inclusion underpin all aspects of work and life and can be powerful levers for success. In this chapter, we want to try and unpack the relationship between diversity, good working practices and the effective provision of goods and services; and this is how we start to make sense of, what we have termed, *The Transient Diversity Dynamic.*

The challenge here is a bit of a paradox – just as soon as we think that we have understood Diversity, we come to realise that there is yet another layer underneath. However, the solution to this conundrum lies in understanding principles much more than simply trying to address just symptoms brought about by a flawed understanding of diversity. What we are alluding to is that diversity is ever changing, and, in fact, one thing that is guaranteed is that the only constant is change. Once upon a time, for example, it was accepted that when a person joined a company after leaving school, college or university, they stayed there until they retired or died. As we saw earlier, it is common practice these days for a person to have had anything up to 5 or even more different employers by the time they retire. Of course, with the abolition of the mandatory retirement age in the UK even retirement age is in a state of flux. This has been the foundation for lots of change in workplace cultures. It is no longer a question of keeping quiet and biding your time; individuals need to be adaptive to changing working dynamics. This is even more so following the globalisation of workforces.

Changing demographics

Today there is far more movement both within a country and across borders than ever before in Human history. In London alone there are over 300 languages spoken in schools[55] with more than 100 different languages spoken in virtually every London Borough.[56] Additionally there is an aging workforce and, in certain areas, a skills shortage in spite of the fact that people are living longer.

Workplace and service cultures, and expectations, are changing faster than ever before.

It is no longer valid to assume that somebody who is aged 60 is computer illiterate. Equally it has become commonplace to see 18 month old toddlers comfortably managing their parents' tablet. However, notwithstanding these advances, human psychology has difficulty keeping up with such rapid change and still often prefers the *devil you know....*

This can often lead to unconscious and inherent bias in decision making.

Increasing technological aids

With the advances in technology we now have far more capacity to employ a much broader diverse range of people and to serve a similar customer/user base. Especially with the increase in life expectancy, technological advances have proven to be a great facilitator in terms of the retention of staff and customers. For example with the new generation of text to talk and talk to text services many audio and visual impairments do not prevent individuals from working efficiently, effectively and productively.

When we consider service provision, the introduction of automated facilities is now widespread and can be seen around us all the time. For example we no longer need to wait for a person to serve us at a check out point in a supermarket. This allows, for example, someone with a disability who may need more time than others to process their shopping to continue at their own pace without feeling pressured by the checkout representative to rush their packing.

Greater life expectancy

As mentioned earlier, people across the world are generally living longer, largely due to the significant advances in medicine. The United Nations Department of Economic and Social Affairs Population Division produced a paper on World population which confirmed that the population is aging.

In the UK many employers have seen an overall rise in the average age of their workforces. This has led to a need to take a different perspective on workforce planning as there are no longer the same number of people leaving the education system to join the world of work. On the other side of the coin, businesses are also needing to adapt and consider new niche markets for different age groups. When was the last time you saw an advert for a club 18-30 holiday? Mainstream advertising has tended to be focused on family and quality higher end products in terms of holidays; something that has become much more affordable if you have been in paid employment for a number of years.

The advantages of an increasingly aging workforce mean that organisations are able to retain a lot more corporate history and are not experiencing a drain in terms of expertise and historical experience that was once quite common when organisations were downsizing, for example, following a merger or takeover.

Further, with the abolition of the mandatory retirement age, organisations are getting much smarter with considering competency based assessment to ensure that staff can still do the job that they were recruited to do.

Sandwich generation

The Sandwich Generation refers to those within the population who have both elder care and younger care responsibilities. It is not uncommon today to find working adults who need to also plan for the care of parents and their offspring. Some of this is covered in legislation; pregnancy and maternity is now a protected characteristic in UK Law. Age, too, is protected and, indirectly, working adults are protected against 'Discrimination by Association'.

The Sandwich generation has provided employers and service providers with opportunities to explore and implement creative and innovative ways of working which has been facilitated to some extent by the advances in technology. Organisations have demonstrated an ability to respond to and serve customers and service users on a 24/7 basis by introducing more flexible agile working practices which have also benefited employees.

Agile working patterns

Long gone are the days of the 9-5 regime being the only option, and in its place we are seeing employers looking to provide working patterns that will attract the best and most competent employees. Amongst the top ten benefits that new graduates look for are in the arenas of diversity, flexibility and work life balance. Organisations need to be flexible and responsive in order to attract the best talent and greater market share. This has led to new departures in working patterns and customer service. It is not uncommon these days to have a hot desking office. However, as mentioned earlier human psychology is such that change is often met with considerable resistance even though change can lead to very positive outcomes for both staff and customers or service users.

Many organisations seek to capitalise on the benefits by introducing formal agile working policies which consolidate the legal right, in the UK, to request flexible working.

Cultural identity (Second/third generation)

Research has shown that culture and cultural identity are still often the source of unconscious bias even with third and fourth generation communities. For example rates of under achievement amongst African Caribbean, Bangladeshi and other smaller communities are still quite stark even though these communities have been in the UK for a least three generations. This is apparent even in the degree attainment grades of students from such backgrounds.

This challenge will continue as the demographic changes with newer communities joining the population. Often such newer communities are filling essential and vital labour requirements. At the time of the Windrush there was a significant shortage in public transport roles. Today we are seeing a significant shortage of trained nurses and midwives.[57] These shortages, in the short term, can only be filled by recruiting a more diverse workforce which in its self brings about a changing dynamic in terms of culture and cultural identity. It is very useful to be wary of fixed attitudes that can be disparaging towards people who are different or from a culturally different background. By way of example it is a known fact that children who have the same sex parents can often be treated badly by their peers.

Diversity and the bottom line

Much has been made of the business case for Diversity in our aggregated 35 years that we have been working in this field. You only have to look at organisational websites such as *Race for Opportunity*[58] and the *Business Disability Forum*.[59] In more recent times, the then Deputy Mayor of London promoted a seminar (c.2013) about the Diversity Scorecard, which was very well attended and shows how much interest there is in the business case.

Very often, an effort is made to link the business case directly to bottom-line profits. We choose to present a slightly different perspective on the business case, to be seen more as an investment in your people and your organisation. After all, nobody considers the business case for cash flow in a business, but without it a business would very quickly run into difficulties.

So, what does this investment consist of? We would like to think of it as the people flow of your organisation. Without your employees and customers or service users, your business would very quickly cease to exist.

Once upon a time a person was giving a seminar in a very prestigious venue. He pulled out a £50 note and asked if anybody would like it. The majority of the hands in the room went up. He then screwed up the note into a ball and then again asked how many people would want it? Again a similar number of hands went up. This time the speaker threw the ball onto the floor and jumped on it. Again the same question was put to the audience and a similar response was received. He asked the question as to why they would want this note when it had been abused in this way. The answer that came was *because it's a £50 note.*

Of course what the audience really meant was that they recognised the inherent worth of what was in front of them. Had the note been inside an envelope its inherent worth could have been missed easily.

Similarly the inherent worth of our workforce and customer base can only be used to maximum benefit when it is recognised and utilised; it is all about understanding how to maximise and value what is right in front of us. For example, during a recent positive action programme being run for a client organisation, one of the delegates had an idea that appeared to have a lot of value for the organisation. The delegate in question was working in the same department as the head of the function who happened to also be a mentor on the programme. After a conversation with one of the authors of this book, the delegate contacted the head of function introducing himself as a member of the positive action programme and requesting a 30 minute meeting. The Head of function obliged (because of his involvement with the programme) and following the meeting authorised the delegate's proposal which resulted in cost savings of around £250,000 to the organisation. Had the individual not been involved in the positive action programme the idea may never have come to fruition; the line manager may not have (unconsciously) seen beyond the colour of the individual's skin (the envelope)

Whilst we are not saying that every individual in an organisation has the same capability we are saying that where potential exists it is in the organisation's interest to develop it. The spin off benefits include increased loyalty and improved morale, which lead to longer term stability and more motivation to be innovative and creative. To state a well-known leadership phrase *'If you always do what you always did, you always get what you always got'*. A great example of this was the demise of the railways in the United States; business owners thought they were in the train business and failed to realise that were actually in the travel industry. They continued to work on trains and failed to see the advantages of cars and planes because they had failed to recruit a significantly diverse workforce who could have brought in different way of thinking and creativity.

There can be major advantages in our ability to respond to dynamic markets and changing customer bases in order to ratchet up baseline profits. By way of example, when a certain university changed it student intake to incorporate many more students from the Far East, the local shops benefited by stocking foods and other items that originated from the locality of the new students.

If we take a much bigger example, created in c.1998, HSBC Bank increased its appeal to a new market segment when it introduced its South Asian banking units to key areas of the United Kingdom, giving it a significant competitive advantage at a time when markets appeared to be saturated. The business case for diversity is referenced in quadrant 1 of diagram 19.

Diversity and Creating Shared Values

Earlier, we talked about mission, vision and values. When values are simply imposed, there tends to be a level of apathy from employees who are told simply to tow the corporate line. Whilst many organisations have established a set of values, it is advisable for value sets to be reconsidered at each major strategic review (maybe every 3 to 5 years). In all likelihood, value sets are unlikely to change drastically, but each review allows input from all key stakeholders. When people feel that they have been heard and can feel ownership of the organisation's values, there tends to be a much stronger level of loyalty to the organisation and what it represents.

It becomes important, once values are agreed, to ensure that they are widely publicised when the organisation is marketing and recruiting. This way, the organisation seeks to attract those people who are willing to align themselves to the organisation's values. For example in the UK the John Lewis Partnership boasts that they are 'Never knowingly undersold' and this has created a strong loyalty to the John Lewis brand both amongst customers and its workforce.

In our experience of working with organisations, when asked to state their organisational values, individuals often find themselves at a loss. Sometimes, they even tell us that the values are on a wall in their office but they could not tell you *what* they were. This is a classic indicator of an organisation that is likely to be simply task-focused rather than values-led. Recently, we were talking to someone who works in the Financial Services sector, who was very stressed because they had one single focus, which was to maximise the points earned; in UK commercial banking, staff earn points for selling products and services. Each branch, area and region is charged with achieving a targeted number of points.

Many financial institutions have values related to putting the customer first, and yet in this situation, clearly this value was not necessarily shared by the employee because of the pressure placed on them to simply increase sales. The Media recently reported the first significant fine in the UK incurred by a major financial services provider for mis-selling to vulnerable customer groups. Prior to that, in 2008, the world witnessed the near collapse of the banking sector which was largely the result of profiteering over principles.

This clearly points to a misalignment of values and business objectives. Similar situations have been seen in the past where customers who perhaps were not as well educated as others were miss-sold endowment policies. A similar situation precipitated the downfall of a number of predominantly US based banks in the wake of the secondary housing crisis where due regard, in our opinion, was not given to values.

When all stakeholders have buy-in to an organisation's values, there is much less likelihood for the need to resort to remedies involving discrimination, bias and prejudice; values point to the desired and acceptable behaviours expected by all managers, staff and customers. A common and shared value system is the foundation for an environment of mutual dignity and respect wherein individuals can work productively and cooperatively to maximise business and organisational success. It is important to note that such value systems transcend more limited and parochial beliefs, values and attitudes. (See Chapter 1)

Diversity and CSR

Organisations which have a Corporate Social Responsibility (CSR) function will often take up initiatives within communities and situations that have been subject to disadvantage. What, then, does Corporate Social Responsibility actually mean?

The World Business Council for Sustainable Development stated:

> "Corporate social responsibility is the continuing commitment by business to behave ethically and contribute to economic development while improving the quality of life of the workforce and their families as well as of the local community and society at large."[60]

Whilst this definition originated at the turn of the millennium, we consider it still to be valid today. Perhaps we could even think about CSR as community saving returns as it is often regarded as 'Social Value'. Within this definition, we can see that equality, diversity and inclusion are inherent.

We believe, as shown in diagram 19, that CSR attaches to all aspects of business and performance. When customers and service users see good CSR practices within an organisation, this is likely to lead to an organisation becoming an employer and supplier of choice because, amongst other things, it will appeal to individuals' sense of justice and propriety.

The investor base becomes very important for private-sector businesses who are seeking to tap new markets on a regular basis. A very good example of this is the range of 'Fair Trade' products widely available in the majority of supermarkets and can be seen as putting CSR into

Businesses and other organisations rely on ongoing success for their survival. This requires an ability to adapt to changing circumstances and environments by maximising the use of diverse workforces and customer bases

Morals are often regarded as Individualistic, based in broad societal and cultural norms. For Example you will not steal, you will pray 5 times a day, you will not kill another.

The Business imperative	The Moral Imperative
The Legal Imperative	The Ethical Imperative

Recognising that inequality exists and that some organsations / individuals are not aligned to the other three imperatives, then the force of law compels us to eliminate unlawful discrimination and foster good relationships between different people

Ethics are often driven by a moral imperative, and are collective; a set of behaviours belonging to a given group, eg, a political party, a company, a religion. Ethics are about applying morals into the current context.

Diagram 19

practice through its employment of ethical trading strategies and fair trade policies. This creates a link particularly for members of Black and Minority Ethnic communities who may have heritage from those parts of the world.

In terms of both ethical stance and business success, CSR departments are often keen to support sectors of diverse communities that have historically faced discrimination and prejudice. A very good example of this has been seen in the sponsorship of organisations such as African Caribbean Diversity, which has very successfully supported BME students through Summer Schools at Oxbridge.[61]

Diversity and Inclusion

The recurring theme, as you will have gathered by now, is vision, mission and values. Most organisations build their business plans around their vision, mission and values. We have yet to come across a set of corporate mission, vision and value statements that outrightly promote bias and discrimination. Additionally, many organisations have stated that people are their greatest asset.

The assertion is not, for example, that white middle class men are our greatest asset. Inclusion is therefore implicit but does not translate necessarily into an organisation's demographic profile. This then impacts on how we treat customers and staff. This is particularly the case where organisations have felt the need to modernise themselves. Maybe this was one of the primary reasons for the plethora of Equalities legislation in the 60-year period to 2010, which culminated in consolidation through the Equality Act.

Perhaps one very important element of equalities legislation, which is part 3 of the Public Sector Equality Duty (see chapter 6, *Educate or Legislate*), is an aspect that often gets forgotten: Inclusivity. By way of example, gender includes both women and men, even though the majority of cases may relate to unfair treatment of women. Equally, the concept of discrimination by association seeks to include people who themselves are not, for example, gay or disabled, from the effects of adverse treatment. A number of the protected characteristics will apply to every member of the UK population, namely: Race, Sex, Age, and Sexual Orientation.

Furthermore whilst legislation may be aimed at creating a level playing field it is also underpinned by the principals of equity and inclusion: every individual has a right to live and work (and study) free from any form of unlawful discrimination. This is further reinforced in that all of us can claim protection even when someone is discriminating against us simply because they think we have a particular protected characteristic.

Thus, we can see that diversity and inclusion are really inextricably linked. This is referenced against quadrant 4 (the ethical imperative) of diagram 19.

Diversity and Leadership

There is a biblical expression that *God made man in his own image*. When we consider the many versions of God that exist in people's perceptions we can understand that organisational leaders may often have an unconscious desire to recruit leaders in their own image. There is a well known joke which reads,

"When God created man she was just playing around."

If leaders were to recruit only in their own image, we would have a clone culture which can be lacking in innovation and creativity. We have seen over the last 20 years a distinct lack of diversity in the makeup of most boardrooms. Whilst the gender composition amongst the FTSE 100 companies is changing there are a number of other elements of diversity from which boardrooms can benefit. Research conducted by McKinsey and published in February 2015 pointed to significant improvements in performance by having better gender and ethnicity representation on Boards.[62]

Very successful businesses have been led by women; for example, the Body Shop before it was quoted on the Stock Exchange. Unfortunately, such examples are few and far between. Even today we have seen that there is a pay differential of up to 22% between men and women in like-for-like work.[63] Leaders, then, as we have said a number of times, previously carried the brunt of responsibility to ensure that their organisation's practices were fair and equitable for everybody. A common defensive position taken by leaders, particularly in the private sector, is that their business cannot afford to sustain such an egalitarian position, as they would very quickly go out of business. We seek to challenge this perspective because, as we have seen, companies such as Pret-a-Manger have appealed to people's sense of responsibility by sourcing only organic produce.

Leaders need to think about diversity of thought, people, product, place and promotion in order to create organisations that become true 21st-Century models of good practice. It is surprising, therefore, that diversity does not feature regularly in the agendas of most board meetings, but is rather delegated to the HR function. Our experience shows that diversity practices are most fruitful when the diversity and inclusion lead reports directly to the CEO or a Managing Director. Leaders, after all, are the primary shapers of this world and steps that they take to promote diversity and inclusion can have a significant impact. Leaders need to drive all 4 quadrants of diagram 19.

Diversity and Teamwork

Many individuals work in team structures and are required to ensure that both individual and team goals are achieved. For our purposes a team comprises two or more individuals who, in addition to having their individual goals and objectives, are required to work together and collaborate; often providing support and cover in the others' absence.

The effectiveness of any team is always enhanced by common understanding founded on mutual dignity and respect, underpinned by the strategic drivers of the organisation. When a team leader finds a formula that she/he 'likes' there is a tendency sometimes to apply the same set of 'likes' when recruiting future team members. The composition of teams is then not always as diverse as it could be. It is very easy to give dignity and respect to those with whom we share common cultures but less so when it takes an effort. Let's take the example of a new team member who has been appointed through a panel and using competency based recruitment techniques. The person may well have all the requisite skills to undertake the job but finds that their six monthly appraisal indicates that they are under performing. Knowing that the person has the skills to do the job and that satisfactory references were provided, it is reasonable to conclude that the underperformance (in the absence of extraneous circumstances) may well be linked to a lack of belongingness within the team.

Having mutual dignity and respect does not necessarily mean that we, as individuals, have to agree with everything that is presented to us. However when we are unable to integrate members into our team structure, the team productivity and effectiveness can suffer. This is often because of an expectation that the new member should make all the effort to fit in and is indicative of a culture of assimilation, which can stifle innovation and creativity. An example of this may be where we consider the brewing industry. Beer was traditionally brewed by men for men, so most of the brewery teams were composed largely of men. The problem arose when it was recognised that markets were saturated and the only scope for expansion was into the women's market. Beer for women was never really going to become popular if the producers only ever employed men to work in the brewing teams. Similar issues can be identified in a number of sectors, namely Construction, Engineering, Fire & Rescue; and the list goes on.

Simply employing a group of individuals from diverse backgrounds does not necessarily constitute the formation of effective teams. A certain level of commonality needs to be found and built upon. There is a strong need to ensure that the diversity within teams is not merely a token gesture. If the principle of the 'one-organisation culture' has been embedded, then this will provide the appropriate context against which the team can function, working towards common organisational goals and objectives. Of course, individuals do not leave their individuality on the doorstep when they arrive at work, and so it is necessary to engender a culture that is inclusive and recognises the needs and traditions of every individual so that they can give their best in the role.

Team fit, however, is not just about the individual needing to make sacrifices so that they may be accepted by the team. It is very much a two way process where team members also need to be able to give something in order to benefit from the potential gains that the new team member brings with them. Some teams require people with specialist skills which mean that those certain individuals whilst reporting into the same line manager are not necessarily able to support team functionality as described at the beginning of this section. For example someone with low spectrum autism may be very proficient in the technical aspect of a role but may not always have what is deemed to be acceptable social skills. In such circumstances it is beneficial to provide appropriate guidance to team members so that they have a better understanding and can accommodate satisfactorily. Team work is referenced at quadrant 2 (the moral imperative) of diagram 19.

Diversity and the Balanced Scorecard

The concept of the balanced scorecard[64] is not new and in the past has been developed to be used as a tool to measure quantitative results of good equality and diversity practice. What success will look like will be determined by the organisation concerned and can typically include elements such as return on investment, user satisfaction and indirect costs, amongst others.

In fact, many of the equality schemes set up by Public Sector bodies are a form of diversity balance scorecard. The intent of such a process ought to be to look at outcomes rather than outputs. For example, the fact that an organisation may be producing product information in 15 languages is not necessarily a sign of good diversity practice, where it is evident that only 8 of the 15 languages are in regular usage.

If the organisation researched the demography of its customers or service users, and then produced its information in the required number of languages, that is a greater measure of success. A diversity related balanced scorecard is a demonstration of the effective use of finite resources.

In our opinion, there is little point in having an exclusive diversity balanced scorecard if there is not a broader balanced scorecard into which it feeds at the most strategic

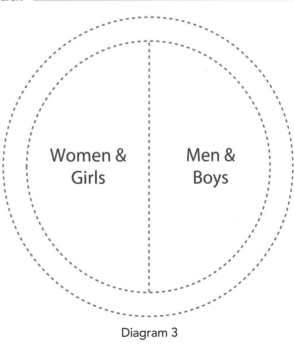

The Individual – Subject to the influence of Values, Beliefs and Attitudes

Diagram 2

levels of the organisation. In this way, diversity becomes one of the measures of success against which the organisation makes itself accountable for diversity and inclusion in line with profitability, productivity, cost containment and maximising business success.

Diversity and the Individual

Diversity exists because we each are individuals. Even if we were to take the example of cloning, we know that clones take on their own characters and personalities even though they share significantly more common traits with their 'parent' and with fellow clones than they would with normal parents and siblings. An organisation is no different, and often there is an unconscious desire in the workplace to surround oneself with clone-like colleagues.

This perpetuates (Unconscious) bias against those individuals who are not so clone-like. Most of us will have heard the story of the ugly duckling who felt alone and isolated until he found himself in the company of swans. We are not all the same, and it is understandable that we often

Women & Girls

Men & Boys

Diagram 3

feel far more comfortable when we are surrounded by people who look like us, talk like us and share our interests. However, a company or an organisation, is a vehicle for business and/or

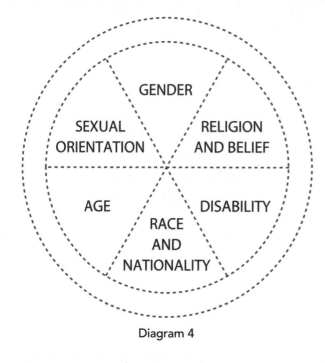

Diagram 4

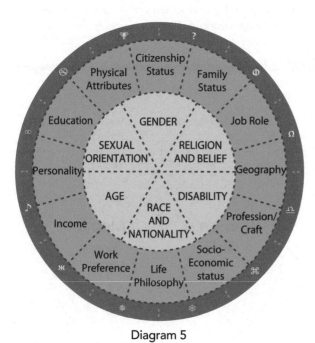

Diagram 5

service provision; all the individuals in the organisation do not need to resemble swans because they will not then be able to identify with and provide appropriate services to the ducks, the geese, the hens and the peacocks.

Let's revisit our diagrams 2, 3, 4 and 5:

These diagrams show us that the individual is the starting point and underpins all the facets of diversity. Of course, we also know that the individual has been subject to conditioning (nurture) since he/she/they was/were in the womb. The individual starts acquiring an identity well before it enters the world of the consumer and the employer. In the current environment of the global marketplace, we see far more acceptance of the individual than perhaps ever before in history.

However, data still suggests that individuals can find it hard to integrate into mainstream communities; *Intelligence for multi ethnic Britain –* A Runnymede Trust report stated that the majority of Black & Minority Ethnic students are more likely to attend a less prestigious university and obtain a lower class of Degree.

Historically, people have been expected to conform to local norms and customs. When this has not happened, it has led to outrage amongst the leaders of society. A classic example of this was Oscar Wilde who ended up enduring prison for a lifestyle that has far more acceptance now than previously.

More recently, Alan Mathison Turing,[65] OBE, FRS, widely considered to be the father of computer science and artificial intelligence, faced a criminal prosecution on account of his sexuality in 1952. He died in 1954, just before his 42nd birthday, from cyanide poisoning. On 10 September 2009, following an Internet campaign, the then British Prime Minister, Gordon Brown, made an official public apology on behalf of the British government for the way in which Turing was victimised by the establishment.

Chapter 10

What We Don't Know Can't Hurt Us? (Unconscious Bias)

"Well, why do I have to do this training?", he complained to himself. "I am perfectly happy with the people I select to work with me; I pride myself on choosing the right people to do the job!"

So far, we have regularly been touching on the manifestation of unconscious bias. What, therefore, is the principal of unconscious bias? If we break the phrase down into its component parts, then:

Unconscious = something that is not conscious. i.e. we are not aware of it in our normal waking state.

Bias = something to which we are positively or negatively attached. i.e. a preference or an aversion.

Most species, whether animal or human, have evolved over time to protect themselves from, initially, the threat of extinction. The human body, and more precisely the brain, has developed accordingly. The Amygdala, a set of neurons, is, we are told, responsible for activating our fight or flight response, a reaction which is triggered unconsciously, based on either a real or an imaginary threat. Consider how one might react to a rope hanging from a tree on a dark night in a jungle. The Amygdala is triggered as there is the potential for that rope to be a poisonous snake.

Daniel Kahneman, in his book, 'Thinking, Fast and Slow',[66] developed the notion of System 1 thinking and System 2 thinking. The first is fast, metaphorical, spontaneous and automatic. It cannot be switched off. By contrast, System 2 is slow, effortful, and requires conscious attention. From this we can deduce that the Amygdala can be considered as part of our System 1 thinking and can often be responsible for our unconscious biases.

Unconscious Bias is a term that has now been circulating for at least 10 years and is seen as a reason behind a lack of Equality, Diversity and inclusion in the workplace and in customer service. The terms 'Unconscious Bias' and 'Implicit Bias' are often ascribed the same meaning and tend to be used interchangeably. However, if we were to look at the two terms more closely, we can recognise that Unconscious bias is just that: unconscious and not accessible by our logical, rational, thinking mind. On the other hand, once awareness is raised, then, strictly speaking it is no longer unconscious but rather, *implicit*. Both unconscious and implicit biases may be regarded as inherent in all individuals and, from the work of Gordon Allport (see Chapter 1, *Identity & Culture: The Basis of Perception*), we can deduce that even children in kindergarten or nursery are subject to it. It manifests in 'Anti-locution' (name calling), and 'Avoidance' (in-groups/outgroups). It does not take long for this to be hard wired into an individuals way of thinking and behaving and this can be seen in things such as the Jesuit saying, 'Give me a child till the age of seven and I will give you the grown man'. Even here, consider the inherent bias in terms of the value attached to the 'man' rather than the woman.

An example of unconscious bias can be seen when, following the World Wars, solders returned from combat, their position as the main breadwinner was threatened and would have created a lot of inner conflict within their unconscious belief systems; suddenly, women were doing the jobs which they (men) previously did, and doing them effectively. However, there was something deep in the recesses of the mind (the Amygdala – a threat to my survival) that did not necessarily allow them to accept this usurpation of their prime position. This then would have been overlaid with the conscious threat men faced from the suffragette movement and so would have activated unconscious strategies to see off the threat (fight) or to avoid it (flight). Whether this threat was real, or imaginary the unconscious, system one thinking, would not recognise the invalidity of it and unconscious, often collective strategies would kick in for 'self preservation'. It would have been detected in the way, for example, careers advice was given to young adults; women were often encouraged to become secretaries as they would 'soon be getting married' and then their husbands could look after them'. As Inequality became more apparent over the years it led to the passing of the Equal Pay Act (1970) and the Sex Discrimination Act (1975) in the UK. In spite of these major pieces of legislation, we can see unconscious bias still reflected in the workplace in 2016; depending on which research is considered, there is still an 11% – 22% differential in favour of men. Unconscious bias can be seen and detected in jokes and banter, which reinforce stereotypes, for example:

Q: "Why do women have smaller feet than men?

A: "So they can get closer to the kitchen sink"

When considered more closely, evidence suggests that female students outperform male students throughout school and university, and yet, are still extremely under-represented in the boardrooms of the FTSE top-100 companies.

If all things were equal, then their performance in studies suggests that they should be the leaders in business and organisational life. To take a simple example, it is very often the norm to buy cars for boys and kitchen sets for girls, and to do so without thinking of the stereotyping that underpins the choice.

By the same token, research shows there to be little difference in the intellectual capability of black children and white children at the age of four years and yet, by the time those same children get to age 16, white children seem to be out performing their black counterparts. Do teachers consciously single out young black students for detrimental treatment? Most, if not all teachers would balk at the thought, it is unthinkable…or is it? System1 processes are so fast and automatic that they may need to be tempered by the slower conscious thinking processes of System 2.

Earlier in this book we saw the impact of our beliefs, values and socialisation (see Chapter1, *Identity & Culture: The Basis of Perception*). For example, at a recent seminar, one of the authors was regularly addressed as 'sir', which would appear very strange to another audience with a different cultural background. To put this into context, in a team of IT professionals, new people were brought in, on secondment from India, to the South West of England. The Indian employees would defer to their team leader by calling him 'Sir'. Very quickly they felt alienated from their colleagues and could not understand why. Upon further investigation it transpired that the white members of the team felt that their Asian colleagues were trying to make them look bad and also seeking the support of the team leader to stay permanently in the UK. With further probing, it transpired that the major evidence they could come up with, to support this stance, was that the Asian colleagues used terms of respect such as 'sir' when speaking to people they considered more senior to themselves.

What is often seen as unconscious bias is more accurately an inherent part of who we are, and have become, as a result of our beliefs, values and attitudes. This creates within us implicit associations of good and bad, right and wrong, acceptable and unacceptable etc. This inherent bias can create an inequitable approach to people who may look different to us, speak differently and/or behave differently. Once we become aware of such implicit bias, it becomes far easier to manage it, should we choose to.

Psychologists, today, have discovered many types of bias which operate through our automatic and involuntary System 1 processing. We have chosen to focus on just a few in this book.

"Like Me" (Affinity Bias)

Human beings have, historically, been very tribal and this breeds a need to be around those with whom we relate. Taking a soccer analogy, we would want to be in the same seating as the others supporting the team we support. We would not only be uncomfortable but perhaps even threatened if our seats were with supporters of the competing team. This is really the crux of affinity bias; the unconscious (and perhaps conscious) bias towards "people who keep us in our comfort zones or, in other words, "people who are like me." This is almost an involuntary response and "people who are not like me," now may pose them a threat, creating an irrational fear. Nobody really wants to be surrounded by people who make them feel uncomfortable.

Here below, is a situation encountered by one of the authors.

Recently, (and keep in mind that he has a North Indian heritage), one of the authors had reason to phone a shoe store for assistance with one of his recent purchases. The woman who answered the phone spoke with an Indian accent and even though I explained my query I felt as though she did not understand what I was saying, but kept asking if I had received an email confirming that my on-line order had been received at the store. I tried to explain that I needed the shoes for an important family wedding that was coming up in a matter of days. I could feel my blood pressure increasing and my patience levels were most definitely not at optimum. Did these people (and notice the term, "these people", I had, unconsciously, grouped this individual into a group of faceless 'foreigners' who would not be able to) grasp the urgency of my need. She told me that she would look to see if they had the style and size I required, in stock. Feeling exasperated, I told her that I would come along that day or the next day to collect. This could be a story about poor customer service, but, perhaps more importantly, this was about me and my response based on the urgency of my situation and my inherent bias about outsourced call centres, even though this person was responding to my call from the store and, no doubt, had received training in responding to customers on the telephone.

If I dig deeper into this story from the angle of affinity bias, I can see that I was not breathing easily, I was feeling tense and frustrated because I had made an assumption that this person would not be able to deal with my query. Later that day, I did pop into the store and queued up at the sales point. I was expecting to be disappointed, but as I was queuing, I could hear the customer service representative speaking to customers in front of me. This person also looked to be of Indian origin, and I found my breathing was easier, my blood pressure seemed to regularise and I questioned myself as to how often had I previously noticed how I am breathing when I am around people who are like me. Equally, it is possible that I am not aware of how my physiology changes (and hence my mental state, too) when I am with or interacting with people different to me, and I am not even aware of why this might be happening. It is entirely possible that this type of automatic response, which manifests as an almost unconscious physiological response (system 1 thinking), then unconsciously makes me less likely to trust those unlike me. This in turn, without my realising it in the moment, may well have consequences in terms of a detrimental impact on decisions I may have to make about, say, interview candidates.

We can deduce from this encounter that, even if we are aware of affinity bias (based on the earlier assumption that we are primarily tribal) this human condition is not going away any

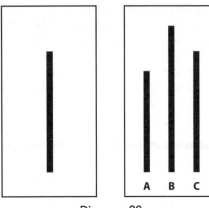

Diagram 20

time soon. Psychologists have suggested that, if we spend a little time reflecting on these types of situation, and then affirm to ourselves that 'I will aim to be more inclusive' it will minimise the risk of Affinity Bias.

"Group Think" (Conformity Bias)

Most people have heard of 'groupthink'. This is where, often unconsciously, there is a desire to agree with the group, often seated in peer pressure, where there is a desire to 'fit in'. This can be reinforced by a strong, often autocratic leader. One of the most famous experiments conducted around conformity bias was originally conducted by Solomon Asch, and has been repeated many times over by others, and has come to be known as the Solomon Asch conformity experiment:

In Asch's experiment 50 male students from Swarthmore College in the USA participated (ie, *real participants*). Amongst every six 'confederates' (actors) Asch introduced a *real* participant, all of whom had to verbally state a response to a visual line judgement test, such as that shown in diagram 20.

It had been agreed with the 'confederates', in advance, as to which responses they would give to a series of cards. Initially the first few responses were to be correct and then the rest of the group were to deliberately all give the same incorrect responses. The responses were to be given aloud with the real participant sitting in the final position of the line-up to give their response.

Across 12 such trials some 75% of participants conformed at least once, and 25% of participant never conformed. In the control group, with no pressure to conform to confederates, less than 1% of participants gave the wrong answer.

When conducting similar experiments, Moscovici (1980) argued that when majorities exert social influence, they produce compliance. That is, individuals will publicly accept the majority view while privately retaining their initial view, motivated by a desire not to appear deviant or to risk possible negative sanctions from the majority, such as ostracism or ridicule.[67]

In the light of such experiments, which can be viewed being conducted on You Tube as late as 2014, we can deduce that such situations could easily occur in the workplace and particularly in panel decisions around selection/promotion where panel members have not been trained to understand the need to follow objective selection processes. For example, when a repeat of the Asch Experiment was conducted, the actors were all told to arrive early and this made the real participant late. As a result, the real participant was told that he had to write down his responses rather than reply verbally. When the real participant did not feel 'exposed' by non-conformity, he was far more likely to give the correct responses in the face of incorrect verbal responses from the actors.

"Self Preservation" (Social Comparison Bias)

Studies have shown that amongst unaware recruiters there can be a tendency to deselect candidates whom they consider will pose a threat to their own area of strength or competence.

In 2010 the *BPS Digest* reported on research conducted by Stephen Garcia and colleagues[68] where they conducted an experiment involving asking undergraduate students to imagine that they were professors. Half the group were asked to imagine they were professors who had produced few but very high quality publications, whilst the other half were asked to imagine that they had produced a high volume of mixed quality publications. They were then presented with a range of CVs for a new Professorship and asked to select their preferred candidate. The candidates' CVs showed either a smaller number of high quality publications or a high volume of mixed quality publications. The results showed that the students tended to select the candidates whose CVs were opposite to their imaginary roles; ie, those students who were asked to imagine they had a fewer number of High Quality publications tended to select candidates with the Higher volume of mixed quality publications and vice versa.

Garcia had virtually identical results in 2 follow up experiments based in real life situations, demonstrating that people tend to select others who do not pose a challenge to their own position or authority. Garcia concluded as follows:

"In sum, the social comparison bias is a broad phenomenon that permeates many different aspects of our organizational and social lives. If we have high standing on one dimension, and if someone threatens to surpass us on that dimension, we become more likely to offer recommendations that are tainted by the social comparison process to prevent that person from besting us in our comparison context. While it is natural to shape these contexts to protect our self-esteem, we must also consider the benefits of overcoming the social comparison bias in these social and organizational settings. In some cases, rising above the social comparison bias might actually lead to a stronger network of social capital and greater opportunity in the long run"

Earlier we talked about the Amygdala and the idea of flight or flight when it comes to self preservation. Unconscious 'Social Comparison' bias can be regarded as the activation of the Amygdala for self-preservation. This is precisely why it makes sense to have a panel of recruiters (such as in a selection centre) which allows candidates to be independently and objectively assessed. Where this is not possible, it is important that the organisation invests in high quality training of recruiters so that such individuals can then counteract any potential bias.

"Find just what you are looking for" (Observational Selection Bias)

One of the authors recently bought a brand new car. He was keen to ensure that he got just the right car for him; one that was reasonably eco-friendly and provided excellent fuel economy. He found the car and chose what he thought was an unusual colour, a metallic grey with a hint of brown in it. No sooner had he selected the car and had it for a day when, all of a sudden, he started seeing loads of cars on the road with the same make and model and, what's more, the same colour! Of course those cars were always there but, until he put his focus on it, he was blind to it. It is in our nature to see things selectively; this is a principle of system 1 (fast) thinking, described earlier. He also remembers riding along with a friend, Tracy Smith, in her car many years ago when he asked her why she kept raising her hand and she said it was a sort of unwritten code between 2CV owners/drivers. The author had not even noticed how many 2CVs there were on the road at that time.

If we were to change the scene and apply this to, say, an interview situation then, without adequate awareness training, we can easily be caught in the trap of observational selection bias and finding ways of justifying the choice of a candidate whom we prefer through recording 'evidence' we have found. This can preclude us from seeing other evidence that might suggest that our choice of candidate is not necessarily the best candidate for the role.

Stereotype Threat

Stereotype threat is a principle that has been widely researched by Claude M Steele[69] and colleagues. It refers to a situation where a person, when reminded of the negative stereotype(s) associated with their characteristic (eg, Ethnicity, gender etc), will find that they then somehow conform to the stereotypical perspective. For example, in Steele and colleagues' research, they chose a group of very athletic black men who were to play golf. Part of the experiment involved the black men being told that historically, golf was a game that white people excelled at and black people did not do so well at it. The outcome was that the self fulfilling prophecy came to pass. Equally, a similar experiment was done with women who were asked to take a math test and were told that historically, men did better at that particular test. The women seemed to do not so well once given that information just before the test. To the contrary, in both situations, where the individuals were given positive messages such as (to the women) the tests were designed to be achievable by both men and women, then the womens' (and the black golfers), results improved significantly.

If we were to extrapolate that situation into a workplace scenario, it would become apparent that, where negative perspectives and, for that matter, negative banter is used against individuals, it can have a quite negative impact on their performance. This also is the case where there are insufficient role models in senior roles that can be emulated by the more junior staff.

This takes us back to almost the beginning of this book where we talked about culture, heritage, beliefs, values and attitudes: "Give me a child till the age of seven and I'll give you the grown man." However, the good news is that all is not lost. Whilst the core of a person's belief system can generate unconscious bias and stereotype threat, the human psyche is so sophisticated that it can find very ingenious ways to work around these, with a little time and effort, of course!

What can be done to Address Inherent Bias and Stereotype Threat?

Most of us like to think that we are fair minded people. Knowledge of unconscious bias is not, in itself, sufficient to address the impact of unconscious bias. This can lead to the idea that others may be subject to unconscious bias, but it could not possibly be applicable to me. Even just introspection and self reflection alone are not sufficient to necessarily recognise inherent biases that are ingrained from childhood, or perhaps earlier (For example, much research has been done that shows how a foetus can be influenced in the womb by the type of music the mother-to-be listens to). One of the authors used to think in the same way until he took the Harvard Business School "Implicit Association Tests"[70] When it comes to ourselves there can often be a bias blind spot and the Harvard research has shown that it is useful to understand our biases. We can then counteract the effects using a combination of the following:

- **Encouraging feedback from colleagues and others** with whom we have working/ professional relationships. It is not always easy to receive (or to give!) feedback of this nature and requires that we develop a culture of feedback within the workplace; where a blame culture exists, it is difficult for individuals to not see feedback except as destructive criticism.

- **Undertake some good quality unconscious bias training**. Whilst there are many on-line courses it is helpful to use a blended approach rather then just relying on a non-responsive methodology where you are unable to ask questions.

- **Make use of affirmations.** Studies have shown that simply re-affirming to your self that you are 'going to be fair and objective with all candidates', has proven to counteract the effects of implicit bias in selection decisions.

- **Take the Implicit Association Tests.** These tests are, at the time of writing, available free from https://implicit.harvard.edu/implicit/takeatest.html. Whilst these tests may not be a perfect measure of unconscious bias, they do provide very strong indications of where our individual biases may sit. They also provide an opportunity for us to reflect on where we may sit with the results that are reported back to us.

- **Anonymise selection decisions** wherever possible and practicable. In September 2000, the American Economic Review reported on research conducted by Claudia Golding and Cecilia Rouse, that the recruitment of women in orchestras increased significantly when auditions were held behind screens so that the recruiters were unable to see the instrumentalists. In September 2014, Hays conducted an experiment in Australia where they sent CVs to some 500 recruiting managers. They then sent the same CVs to another 500 Recruiting managers, but simply changed the names on the CV from Simon to Susan. In reviewing responses of hiring managers of businesses employing more that 500 people, the researchers found that whilst there was agreement that both 'candidates' had similar technical skills, 62% would have been more likely to interview Simon, compared to only 52% more likely to interview Susan.

- **Greater contact with people from diverse backgrounds.** The Amygdala, as we discussed previously, creates an automatic response to any situations where we may feel uncomfortable or threatened. The more we interact with people who are different to us the less will be the need for the activation of the Amygdala. Not only will this help us avoid unconscious bias, but is likely to improve who we are as individuals in terms of being role models, not just at work but in our family and social lives, too.

- **Giving Positive encouragement.** When addressing stereotype threat, we saw, earlier, that giving the right type of messages helps people to increase their performance. This applies to all people regardless of 'protected characteristic'.

- **Being exposed to role models like me.** When considering the impact of stereotype threat, if an individual can point to and see the success of people who look like them, speak like them etc, it will provide an unconscious boost to the given individuals levels of self esteem and self confidence. This can then be focused into conscious awareness, too.

- **Attaching yourself to success.** It has been found that, in order to counteract the effects of stereotype threat, it is a great idea for individuals to build up their own actual and desired profiles. So, for example, writing a pen portrait of how an individual sees themselves in 5 or 10 years time and then regularly reflecting on that has been known to counteract negative stereotype threats.

Chapter 11

The Journey is More Important Than the Destination

"Where do you see yourself in five years time?", asked her line manager at her annual review. I wondered whether I should really tell him what was going on in my mind; that unless the organisation takes action to change some of the existing status quo I am probably going to be doing the same thing as I am doing today…

In this book we have taken you on a whistle stop tour of Equality, Diversity and Inclusion, together with a meander through some of the pitfalls we have seen and often experienced ourselves.

Often, everyday folk just like you and us can get very perplexed when we have to navigate through Equality, Diversity and Inclusion and yet we do not have a map to assist us.

To take an analogy, one moment we are driving along a perfectly clear road; we know the rules and observe the road signs. The problem is that every so often, the fog descends and we feel that we cannot see even 1 metre in front of us. Hopefully, Demystifying Diversity, goes some way towards clearing some of the fog that surrounds this arena of work and customer service. Ultimately, this is all about three key rules:

Know your people

Know your people

Know your people

Such knowledge, when used wisely, will mean that we get it right far more often than we get it wrong.

Enjoy your journey…

Reference

1 Source: https://www.gov.uk/government/uploads/system/uploads/attachment_data/file/218497/employment-trib-stats-april-march-2011-12.pdf
2, 3 *Maslow Abraham H*, A Theory of Human Motivation. ISBN-13: 978-1614274377
4 *Morris Massey*, What You Are Is Where You Were When... Again! ISBN-13: 978-1561062157
4a The principle character in the Harry Potter series, written by J.K.Rowling
5 The Nature of Prejudice, by Gordon Allport, ISBN 9780686950073
6 http://en.wikipedia.org/wiki/Morris_Massey
7 The concept of a 'Significant Emotional Event' was presented in the Seven Habits of Highly Effective People by Steven Covey
8 Enoch Powell's 'Rivers of Blood' speech – source: http://www.martinfrost.ws/htmlfiles/rivers_blood2.html
9 Approximately 10 per cent of cases of anorexia are reported by men.
10 The Springboard Women's Development Programme is a development course for women. Developed originally for the BBC, the Springboard Women's Development Programme has now been successfully used by over 180,000 women world-wide.
11 History of Migration, James, S. Peoples of Britain. 2006. http://www.bbc.co.uk/history/ancient/prehistory/ Kershen, A. Moving here - 200 years of migration to England. 2006. http://www.movinghere.org.uk/ BBC. Short history of immigration. 2006. http://news.bbc.co.uk/hi/english/static/in_depth/uk/2002/race/ short_history_of_immigration.stm BBC. British timelines. 2006. http://www.bbc.co.uk/history/interactive/timelines/
12 Our experience in using this exercise with many groups has shown that when 'white' people are asked to find stereotypes to describe themselves they found it quite difficult to fill in the gaps.
13 Source: www.ifrc.org - International Federation of the Red Cross and Red Crescent Societies.
14 TRACC is a registered trademark and copyright of Demystifying Diversity
15 When an organisation claims to be 'representative' it is often referring to absolutes, e.g., 9% of our workforce is from a BME background. Proportionality, then it is about representation across all levels of the organisation.
16 ©*Socio-diversity* is the copyright of Demystifying Diversity and its authors.
17 Recruitment decisions are based on a person's ability to do the job
18 For example; Rac*ist*, Sex*ist*, Islam*ist*, Age*ist* etc.
19 https://www.gov.uk/government/uploads/system/uploads/attachment_data/file/295833/Analysis_of_the_Gender_Pay_Gap.pdf
20 (source: Study commissioned by Multi-Cultural Communications (MCC), Weber Shadwick's specialists - 2007)
21 *A Peacock in the land of Penguins*, by B J Gallagher and Warren H Schmidt
22 By way of example, the fact that someone may have attended the same Public School as the assessing manager or be a member of the same golf club or a supporter of the same football team, does not necessarily make them suitable for the role although they may well find an affinity with the assessor as a result of such association. In the absence of appropriate recruiter training, such an affinity may well determine whether or not the person is offered the job.

23 Definition taken from the Cambridge English Dictionary

24 http://www.mcdonalds.co.uk/people/join-the-team/join-the-team.shtml

25 http://www.boots-uk.com/Corporate_Social_Responsibility/Workplace/Diversity.aspx

26 http://www.tesco-careers.com/home/working/diversity

27 http://www.starbucks.com/about-us/company-information/diversity-at-starbucks

28 http://www.nextplc.co.uk/corporate-responsiblity/our-people.aspx

29 http://www.dominos.uk.com/people/equal_opportunities.aspx

30 http://www.mypeoplebiz.com/thorntons-careers/equality.aspx

31 http://mothercare.hemscottir.com/our-people

32 http://corporate.marksandspencer.com/mscareers/careers_about/our_diversity

33 See report entitled *Literacy Changes Lives*, produced by the Literacy Trust.

34 Men are from Mars Women are from Venus by John Gray 1992

35 School's ban on boy's cornrows is 'indirect racial discrimination'
High court rules against London secondary school after boy was refused entry for breaching ban on 'gang-related' hairstyles
Ban on 'gang culture' haircuts in school is 'indirect racial discrimination', judge rules.
A London school's decision to ban hairstyles it says have become associated with gang culture has resulted in 'unlawful, indirect racial discrimination which is not justified', a court has ruled.

36 David Cameron makes a play for the female vote: http://www.dailymail.co.uk/femail/article-2056126/Samantha-tells-Calm-dear–David-Cameron-makes-play-female-vote.html#ixzz1cY8lCtjh
http://www.dailymail.co.uk/femail/article-2056126/Samantha-tells-Calm-dear–David-Cameron-makes-play-female-vote.html#ixzz1cY82MLiC

37 http://news.bbc.co.uk/sport1/hi/football/15548056.stm

38 Ralph Waldo Emerson, American Poet, Lecturer and Essayist (1803-1882)

39 Source: Office of National Statistics march 2012

40 http://www.businessdisabilityforum.org.uk/about-us/news/press-release-uk-businesses-miss-out-on-1-8-billion-a-month-as-disabled-people-walk-away-from-poor-service/#sthash.JBQphFPF.dpuf

41 http://www.supremecourt.gov.uk/decided-cases/docs/UKSC_2012_0065_Judgment.pdf

42 http://www.open.ac.uk/ousa/sites/www.open.ac.uk.ousa/files/files/OU_Student_Charter.pdf

43 http://www.instituteofcustomerservice.com/1849-2147/Establishing-a-customer-charter–code-of-conduct.html

44 http://www.natwest.com/global/customer-charter.ashx

45 first, The Guardian; second, The Telegraph.

46 http://www.official-documents.gov.uk/document/cm74/7431/7431.pdf

47 At the time of writing, the notable exception to this rule is in the selection of the UK parliamentary candidate shortlists, which will be in force until proportionality has been achieved

48 Disciplinary and grievance procedures ISBN 978 0 11 706728 8

49 http://www.port.ac.uk/accesstoinformation/policies/humanresources/filetodownload,13116,en.pdf

50 "I" refers to Individual(s)

51 In a one-culture organisation an individual would be expected to fall in line and to *put up and shut up*, whereas a one-organisation culture allows a variety of ways for individuals to coexist and thrive for the benefit of both team and organisational success.

52 The material for this case study has been taken from *Secrets & Big News*, ISBN: 9780992898403, with the permission of the author

53 http://www.youtube.com/watch?v=qbC4irVmsXU

54 BBC.co.uk-Languages across Europe

55 Source London Evening Standard 30th January 2013

56 http://www.huffingtonpost.co.uk/cathy-warwick/midwife-shortage_b_2519344.html

57 race.bitc.org.uk/

58 www.businessdisabilityforum.org.uk/

59 http://www.wbcsd.org/web/publications/csr2000.pdf

60 Oxbridge is a common name for University of Oxford and Cambridge respectively

61 http://www.mckinsey.com/Insights/Organization/Why_diversity_matters?cid=other-eml-
    alt-mip-mck-oth-1501

62 When we talk about like for like work we taking a comparison of the actual tasks and role
    description as opposed to the title of the role.

63 http://www.balancedscorecard.org/BSCResources/AbouttheBalancedScorecard/tabid/55/
    Default.aspx

64 http://en.wikipedia.org/wiki/Alan_Turing

65 Thinking, Fast and Slow, Daniel Kahneman *ISBN*-13: 978-0141033570

66 Source - http://www.radford.edu/~jaspelme/_private/gradsoc_articles/individualism_collectivism/
    conformity%20and%20culture.pdf

67 Garcia, S., Song, H., and Tesser, A. (2010). Tainted recommendations: The social comparison
    bias. *Organizational Behavior and Human Decision Processes*, 113 (2), 97-101 DOI: 10.1016/
    j.obhdp.2010.06.002

68 "Whistling Vivaldi: How Stereotypes Affect Us and What We Can Do (Issues of Our Time)"
    by Claude M Steele.